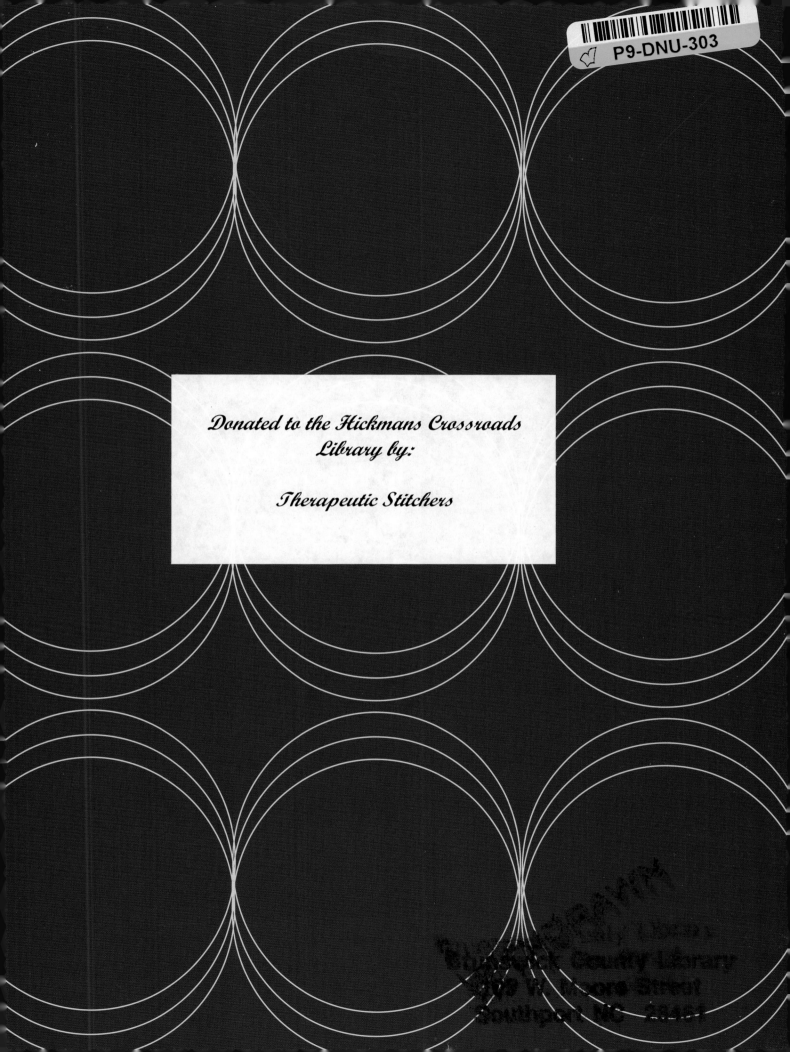

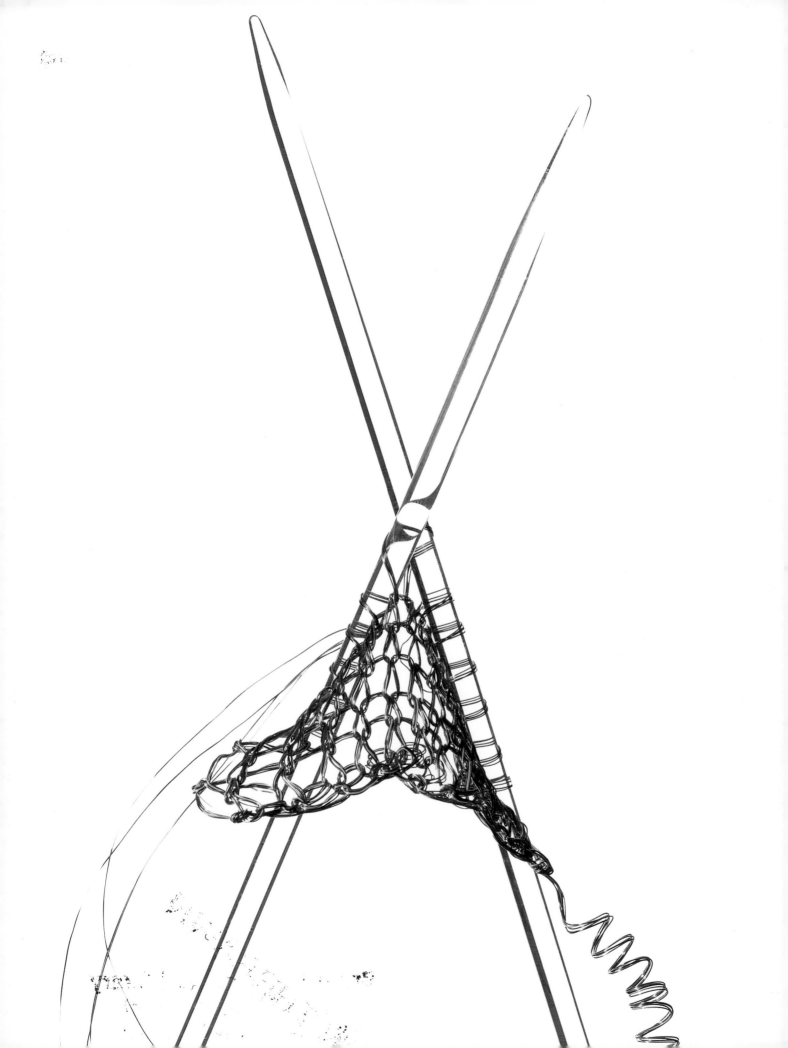

twist + loop

dozens of jewelry designs to knit and crochet with wire

annie modesitt

POTTER
CRAFT

new york

Copyright © 2006 by Annie Modesitt

Published in the United States by Potter Craft,
an imprint of the Crown Publishing Group,
a division of Random House, Inc., New York.
www.crownpublishing.com
www.clarksonpotter.com

POTTER CRAFT and CLARKSON N. POTTER are trademarks,
and POTTER and colophon are registered trademarks
of Random House, Inc.

Portions of this work previously appeared in **Confessions of a Knitting Heretic**
(South Orange, NJ: Mode Knit Press, 2004).

Library of Congress Cataloging-in-Publication Data

Modesitt, Annie.
Dozens of jewlery designs to knit and crochet with wire / Annie Modesitt. — 1st ed.
p. cm.
Includes bibliographical references and index.
ISBN-13: 978-0-307-34019-1 (alk. paper)
1. Jewelry making. 2. Wire craft. I. Title.
TT212.M63 2006
745.594'2--dc22

2006016994

ISBN-10: 0-307-34019-8
ISBN-13: 978-0-307-34019-1

Printed in China

Design by Lauren Monchik
Photography by Bella Borsodi

1 3 5 7 8 9 10 7 6 4 2

First Edition

For Gerry, Hannah, and Max—the best things
that have ever happened to me.
And for my students,
those I've met and those I've yet to meet.

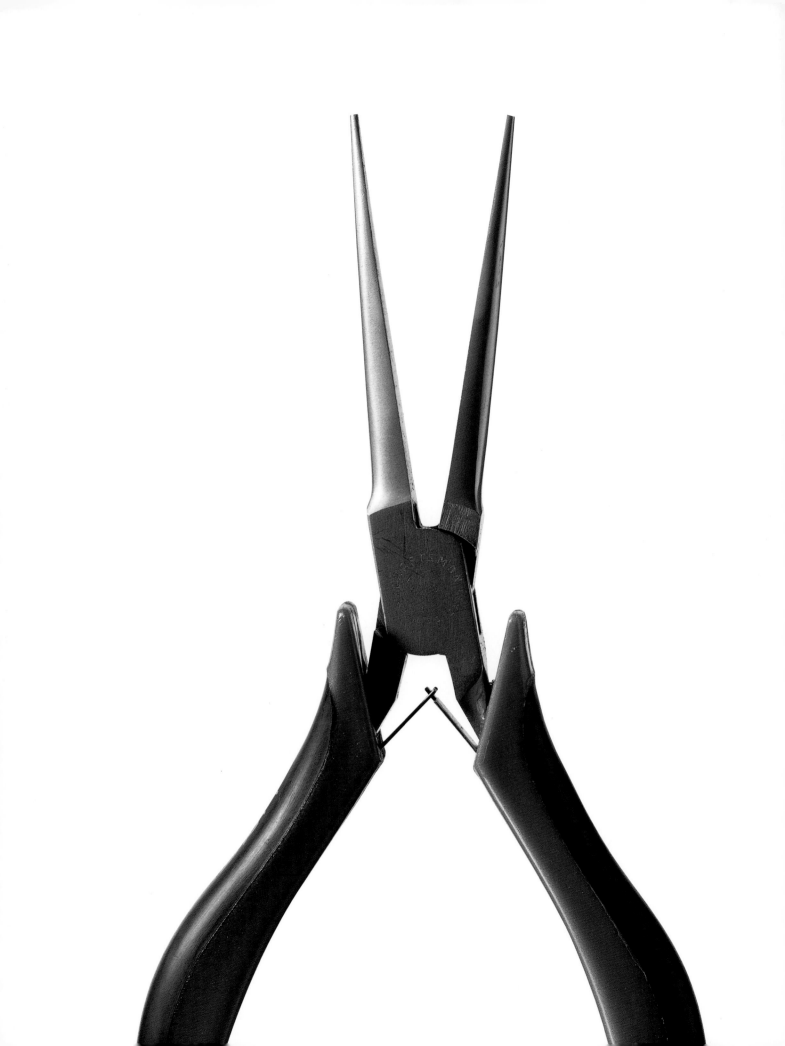

INTRODUCTION: WHY KNIT WITH WIRE?

The most frequent comment I hear when I explain to folks that I knit with wire is, "Wire! Why?" A close second is, "Wire? Cool!" And there is the answer to the first question: I knit with wire because it's cool.

Since we were kids we've loved making things that are neato, cool, groovy, rad—whichever adjective suits your decade. I knit with wire because it's unusual, it's beautiful, and I can make things with wire that I couldn't find anywhere else.

The delight I feel when I see a sweater and know that I can make it is doubled when I realize that I can also make beautiful jewelry pieces for myself and my friends!

Wire is quite different from plant and animal fibers. It lacks flexibility; it can be brittle; it can damage needles and may be rough on the hands. But all the suffering is worth it because wire-knit fabric is extraordinary—it looks different than any other knit fabric.

Beads, shells, and stones all slide along wire stitches like disks on an abacus, creating movement even when the fabric is still. Wire knitting sparkles; it shines and glimmers. When I wear a jewelry piece I have knit, I feel adorned. When I give a wire-knit cuff or necklace as a gift, I am giving something unique and quite unlike any other knit gift I could give.

Knitting with wire is cool—not in the fashion-of-the-minute meaning of the word—but cool because it is fun and joyful, and it gives us a new vocabulary for expressing our artistic selves.

When I look at wire knitting, I feel as if I'm seeing the skeleton of the fabric— the pared-down, naked framework that IS knitting. The stitches have their own strength; they stand on their own in beautiful simplicity.

CHAPTER 1 NECKLACES

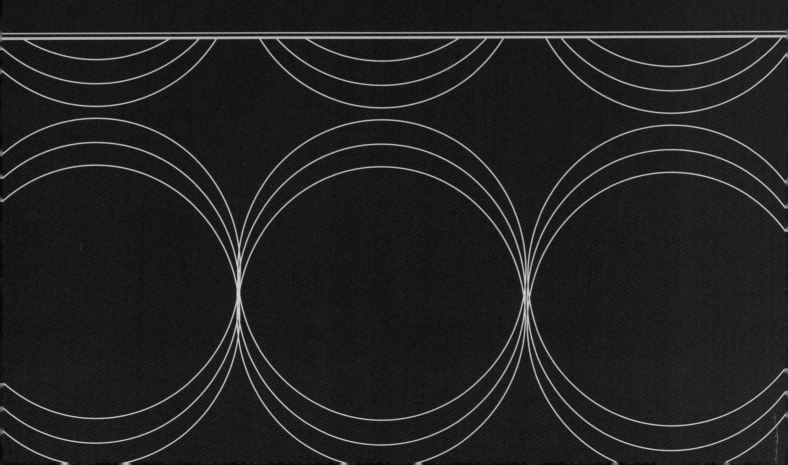

The most important thing to remember when fashioning a piece of jewelry to wear around the neck is to make it comfortable. The wire should be of high quality, and it shouldn't irritate the skin or cause discoloration. Some people have dermatological reactions to certain types of metal—it's good to find out before you present a friend with a painstakingly crafted gift made of a material the recipient can wear! Stranding ribbon or soft fiber along with the wire as you knit is one way to make a necklace more comfortable. Using clear nail polish to dab points on the necklace that may be irritating is another good tip.

very simple wire necklace

Estimated time: Bead stringing, 15 minutes; Knitting, 30 minutes

before you begin

String beads on wire in the foll manner: String all small iridescent beads, then alternate larger beads (1 blue, 1 green) until all are used.

knit

Using any CO method and larger needles, CO 1 st, sl 1 bead onto needle, [CO 2 sts, sl 1 bead onto needle] 17 times, CO 1 st—18 large beads, 36 sts.

row 1 Change to smaller needles. [K1, sl 1 bead onto needle] across to last st, k1.

Block piece on needle.

With 1 strand each of wire and spun silk yarn, and leaving a 30" (76cm) tail of yarn at start of row, BO all sts using whichever method you prefer.

finishing

Block piece by pulling gently from top to bottom, then back and forth from side to side, until all sts seem to have a similar size and shape. Position necklace to determine desired length of neck strands. Attach optional hook-and-loop finding to end of yarn by pulling strands through loops on finding, then securing the leather to itself by wrapping tightly with a 12" (30.5cm) piece of wire.

Wrap wire ends around yarn join at top edges of necklace. Twist, coil, and crimp wire ends to wrong side of necklace to finish, being careful not to crush any glass beads with your pliers.

SKILL LEVEL
K 1 Beginner

SIZE
One size

FINISHED MEASUREMENTS
Varies

MATERIALS
15yds (14m) gold
Artistic Wire, 24 gauge

2yds (2m) Spun sari silk yarn
(Himalayan Yarn)

9 blue pressed glass beads,
size 6 (8mm)
(Blue Moon Beads)

9 green pressed glass
beads, size 6 (8mm)
(Blue Moon Beads)

35 green iridescent beads,
size 2 (2.5mm)
(Blue Moon Beads)

Gold hook-and-loop finding
(optional)

Size 6 (4mm) and size 8
(5mm) knitting needles

NOTIONS
Sewing thread to match silk
yarn, sewing needle
(optional)

SIZE
One size

FINISHED MEASUREMENT
21" (53.5cm)

MATERIALS
10yds (9m) red (#14)
Artistic Wire, 22 gauge

16 shell beads, size 1"
(2.5cm) (The Bead Hut)

Copper toggle finding
(Multi Creations NJ, Inc.)

Size I (5.5mm) crochet hook

chain shell necklace

Estimated time: Bead stringing, 15 minutes; Crocheting, 30 minutes

before you begin

String all 16 beads onto the wire.

crochet

Ch 2, [sl bead onto hook, pull next lp until it is 1" (2.5cm) long (or as long as bead), ch 1 to secure bead, ch 1] 16 times.

finishing

Cut wire, leaving a 5" (12.5cm) tail. Use tails to add findings (see Finishing, page 110); twist, coil, and crimp wire to complete piece.

three-strand very simple crocheted necklace

Estimated time: Bead stringing, 30 minutes; Crocheting, 1 hour

SKILL LEVEL
C 1 Beginner

SIZE
One size

FINISHED MEASUREMENT
18" (45.5cm)

MATERIALS
30yds (27.5m) natural (#10) Artistic Wire (A), 28 gauge

5yds (4.5m) natural (#10) Artistic Wire (B), 20 gauge

204 copper-lined aqua glass seed beads, size 6/0 (Ambrosia Arts)

Copper toggle finding (Multi Creations NJ, Inc.)

Size E (3.5mm) crochet hook

before you begin
String all 204 beads onto wire A.

crochet
short strand With A, leaving a 6" (15cm) tail, ch 2, [sl bead onto hook, holding bead against hook with right finger, ch 1] 64 times, ch 2. Break wire, leaving a 6" (15cm) tail.

medium strand Work as for short strand, but work 68 beads into piece.

long strand Work as for short strand, but work 72 beads into piece.

Block pieces by gently pulling from end to end, slowly turning the chain as you pull so that if the chain has become twisted, it gently straightens out. Continue working in this way, pulling and straightening each strand until they lay flat when held against the throat.

Line up the ends of all 3 strands and twist, coil, and crimp the 3 wire tails tog to finish one end. Being careful not to twist or inadvertently braid the strands tog, rep with the other end.

finishing
Thread a 9" (23cm) piece of B through the last bead in each strand at one end of the necklace. Fold this strand in half and twist the ends tog, creating a very strong twisted wire. Clip this twisted wire so that it's roughly ⅝" (1.5cm) long. Sl the eye of a toggle onto this twisted wire, then coil the end of the wire very tightly, securing the toggle in place, and crimp the twisted wire against its base.

Rep for opposite end of necklace with matching toggle loop.

If necessary, dot with a bit of clear nail polish to prevent scratching.

pink pearl shell necklace

Estimated time: Bead stringing, 1hour; Knitting, 1 hour

before you begin

On wire A, string 32 white rice pearls, 40 freshwater pearls, and 60 white rice pearls.

On wire B, string 32 pink rice pearls, 32 brown shells, 40 pink shells, and 60 pink rice pearls.

knit

Work a slip knot by holding 1 strand each of A and B tog. Sl this onto the larger needle and, using the long-tail method, CO 40 more sts as foll: [sl 2 pink and 2 white pearls onto needle, CO 1 st, sl 2 pink pearls onto needle, CO 1 st, sl 2 pink and 2 white pearls onto needle, CO 1 st, sl 2 white pearls onto needle, CO 1 st] 10 times—41 sts, 60 pink and 60 white pearls.

row 1 (RS) With B, knit.
row 2 (WS) [K1, sl pink shell onto needle] across to last st, k1.
row 3 With A, knit.
row 4 [K1, sl pearl onto needle] across to last st, k1.
row 5 With B, [k2, k2tog-L, k1] across to last st, k1—33 sts.
row 6 [K1, sl brown shell onto needle] across to last st, k1.
rows 7 & 9 With B, knit.
row 8 Purl.
row 10 [P1, sl pearl onto needle] across to last st, p1.
row 11 With A, [k1, sl pearl onto needle] across to last st, k1.
row 12 Purl.

Block piece on needle.

Leaving a 30" (76cm) tail of linen yarn and holding yarn and gold wire tog, BO all sts loosely using larger needle. Leave a 30" (76cm) length of linen and a 5" (12.5cm) length of wire at the end of the BO.

SKILL LEVEL
K 2 Easy

SIZE
One size

FINISHED MEASUREMENTS
2" (5cm) wide, 9" (23cm) along upper edge, 13" (33cm) along lower edge

MATERIALS
100yds (91.5m) silver Artistic Wire (A), 26 gauge

100yds (91.5m) gold Artistic Wire (B), 26 gauge

30yds (27.5m) natural (#203) Block Island Blend linen yarn (Halcyon Yarn)

92 pink rice pearls, size 4mm (The Bead Hut)

92 white rice pearls, size 4mm (The Bead Hut)

32 brown shell beads, size 6mm (The Bead Hut)

40 freshwater pearls, size 8mm (The Bead Hut)

40 pink shell beads, size 10mm (The Bead Hut)

Size 8 (5mm) and size 6 (4mm) knitting needles

Size F (3.75mm) crochet hook

NOTIONS
Sewing thread to match linen, sewing needle, hook-and-loop finding (optional)

SPECIAL STITCHES USED
LTCO (see pages 93–94), k2tog-L (see page 101), k2tog BO (see page 105)

finishing

Block piece by pulling gently from top to bottom, then back and forth from side to side, until all sts seem to have a similar size and shape. Make a crocheted ch with linen ends to create a firmer strand around neck. Position necklace to determine desired length of neck strands. Attach hook-and-loop finding to ends of strands, sewing to the linen with matching thread. Wrap thread tightly around linen and trim end at wrapping point; knot and cut thread.

Wrap wire ends around linen join at top edges of necklace. Twist, coil, and crimp wire ends to wrong side of necklace to finish, being careful not to crush any pearls or shells with your pliers.

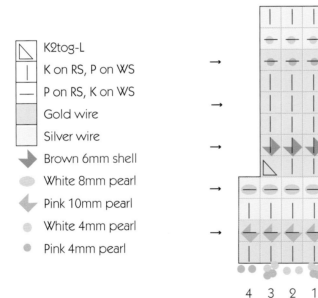

K2tog-L

| K on RS, P on WS

— P on RS, K on WS

Gold wire

Silver wire

Brown 6mm shell

White 8mm pearl

Pink 10mm pearl

White 4mm pearl

Pink 4mm pearl

In the same way that studying a new language can teach us about syntax and grammar in our native tongue, working with wire can educate us about conventional knitting techniques. Seeing the bare bones of a stitch worked in wire helps us understand that knitting is simply a series of loops and how we manipulate, twist, and finish those loops is what encompasses all knitting techniques. We can carry the lessons of wire over to wool, cotton, or the magnificent Artyarn Silk Ribbon and Himalayan Sari Silk (shown right).

falling water necklace

Estimated time: Bead stringing, 1 hour, 15 minutes; Knitting, 1½ hours

before you begin
String beads in the foll order:

66	gold seed beads
33	yellow square beads
33	4mm aquamarine chips
49	gold seed beads
8	green/yellow/blue glass disk beads
16	gold seed beads
210	(approx) iridescent beads
18	green/blue glass disk beads
111	(approx) iridescent beads
37	6–8mm aquamarine chips
111	(approx) iridescent beads

knit
row 1 With larger needle and using the long-tail method, CO 1 st, [sl approx 3 beads onto needle, CO 1 st] 36 times—37 sts.

row 2 (WS) [K1, sl 1 aquamarine chip onto needle] across to last st, k1.

row 3 (RS) [P1, sl approx 3 beads onto needle] across to last st, p1.

row 4 K1, [sl 1 glass disk onto needle, k2] across.

row 5 Rep row 3.

row 6 Slipping approx 3 beads onto needle between each st worked (including decreases), [k5, k2tog-R, k5, k2tog-R, k4] twice, k1—33 sts.

row 7 P1, [sl 1 seed bead onto needle, p2] across.

row 8 K2, [sl 1 glass disk onto needle, k4] across, ending last rep k3 instead of k4.

row 9 Rep row 7.

row 10 K1, [sl 1 seed bead onto needle, k1] across.

row 11 P1, [sl 1 aquamarine chip onto needle, p1] across.

row 12 K1, [sl 1 square bead onto needle, k1] across.

row 13 P1, [sl 1 seed bead onto needle, p1] across.

row 14 K1, [sl 1 seed bead onto needle, k1] across.

SKILL LEVEL
K 4 Advanced

SIZE
One size

FINISHED MEASUREMENTS
2½" (6.5cm) wide, 7½" (19cm) along upper edge, 11½" (29cm) along lower edge

MATERIALS
80yds (73m) green-coated Artistic Wire, 26 gauge

15yds (14m) light green (#120) Deco-Ribbon (Crystal Palace Yarns)

131 silver-lined gold glass seed beads, size 6/0 (Blue Moon Beads)

33 yellow square glass beads, size 4mm (Blue Moon Beads)

37 aquamarine chips, size 4mm (Just Bead It)

37 aquamarine chips, size 6–8mm (Just Bead It)

8 green/yellow/blue glass disk beads, size 10mm (Blue Moon Beads)

18 green/blue glass disk beads, size 10mm (Blue Moon Beads)

450 (approx) green iridescent glass beads, size 2mm (Blue Moon Beads)

Size 8 (5mm) and size 6 (4mm) knitting needles

NOTIONS
Sewing thread to match ribbon, sewing needle, hook-and-loop finding (optional)

SPECIAL STITCHES USED
LTCO (see pages 93–94), k2tog BO (see page 105)

Block on the needle.

Holding wire and 1 strand of ribbon tog, leaving a 30" (76cm) tail of ribbon at start of work, BO all sts using the k2tog BO method.

finishing

Block piece by pulling gently from top to bottom, then back and forth from side to side, until all sts seem to have a similar size and shape. Make a crocheted ch with ribbon ends to create a firmer strand around the neck. Position necklace to determine desired length of neck strands. Attach hook-and-loop finding to ends of strands, sewing to the ribbon with matching thread. Wrap thread tightly around ribbon and trim end at wrapping point; knot and cut thread.

Wrap wire ends around ribbon join at top edges of necklace. Twist, coil, and crimp wire ends to wrong side of necklace to finish, being careful not to crush any glass beads with your pliers.

◤ Ktog BO

● 6/0 silver-lined glass gold beads

■ 4mm square yellow beads

⬥ 4mm aquamarine chips

❧ 2mm green iridescent glass beads

⬥ 6–8mm aquamarine chips

◎ 10mm dia green/yellow/blue glass circle beads

◉ 10mm dia green/blue glass circle beads

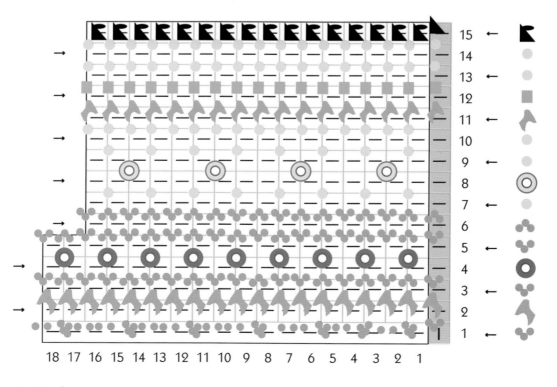

SIZE
One size

FINISHED MEASUREMENTS
2½" (6.5cm) wide, 7" (18cm)
along upper edge, 9½"
(24cm) along lower edge

MATERIALS
100yds (91.5m) amethyst
(#S18) Artistic Wire (A),
30 gauge

100yds (91.5m) purple
Artistic Wire (B), 30 gauge

30yds (27.5m) natural
(#203) Block Island Blend
linen yarn (Halcyon Yarn)

91 silver-lined gold glass
seed beads, size 6/0
(Ambrosia Arts)

39 brown coconut shell
beads, size 8mm

91 bronze opaque glass
seed beads, size 6/0
(Ambrosia Arts)

32 cream pearls, size 6mm
(The Bead Hut)

39 olive top-drilled pearls,
size 6mm (The Bead Hut)

Size D (3.25mm) crochet
hook

NOTIONS
Sewing thread to match
linen, sewing needle, hook-
and-loop finding (optional)

SPECIAL STITCHES USED
Sc (see page 108),
hdc (see page 119),
sc2tog (see page 120)

crocheted pearl &
coconut shell necklace

Estimated time: Bead stringing, 1hour; Crocheting, 1 hour

before you begin

On wire A, string 31 gold beads, 39 coconut shell beads, and 60
gold beads.

On wire B, string 31 bronze beads, 32 cream pearls, 39 olive pearls,
and 60 bronze beads.

crochet

Work a slip knot by holding 1 strand of A and B wires tog. Create
foundation ch as foll: [Ch 1, sl 2 gold and 2 bronze beads onto
hook, ch 1, sl 2 gold beads to hook, ch 1, sl 2 gold and 2 bronze
beads onto hook, ch 1, sl 2 bronze beads onto hook] 10 times—40
sts, 60 gold and 60 bronze beads.

row 1 (WS) With A, ch 1, sc in each st across, turn.
row 2 (RS) Ch 1, sc in first st, [sl coconut shell onto hook, working
behind shell, sc in next st] across, turn.
row 3 (WS) With B, ch 2, hdc tbl in each st across, turn.
row 4 (RS) Ch 1, sc between each hdc of prev row, turn—39 sc.
row 5 (WS) Ch 1, [sl olive pearl onto hook so it hangs toward the
front of work, sc in next st] across, turn.
row 6 (RS) Ch 1, sc in first 4 sts, [sc2tog, sc in next 3 sts] across,
turn—32 sc.
row 7 (WS) Ch 1, [sl cream pearl onto hook so it hangs toward the
front of work, sc in next st] across, turn.
rows 8, 9 & 10 With A, ch 1, sc in each st across, turn. Both strands
are now at start of RS row.
row 11 (RS) Working with both strands at once, ch 1, sc in first st, [sl
1 gold and 1 bronze bead onto hook, sc in next st] across. Fasten off
wires, leaving a 5" (12.5cm) tail.
row 12 With linen, ch 60. With RS facing, join to row 11 and sc
across all 32 sts at top of necklace, ch 60. Fasten off.

finishing

Block piece by pulling gently from top to bottom, then back and
forth from side to side, until all sts seem to have a similar size and
shape. Position necklace to determine desired length of neck strands.
Attach hook-and-loop finding to ends of strands, sewing to the linen
with matching thread. Wrap thread tightly around linen and trim end
at wrapping point; knot and cut thread. Twist, coil, and crimp wire
ends to wrong side of necklace to finish, being careful not to crush
any pearls or shells with your pliers.

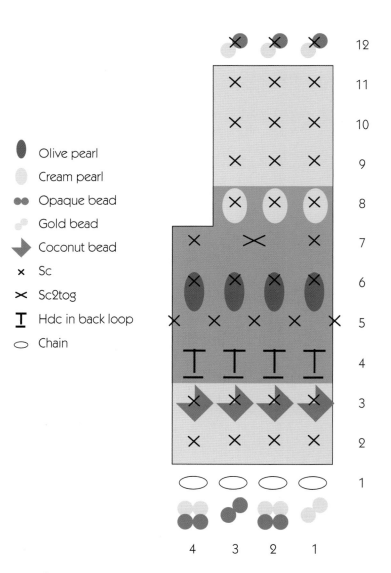

Olive pearl

Cream pearl

Opaque bead

Gold bead

Coconut bead

× Sc

✕ Sc2tog

I Hdc in back loop

⬭ Chain

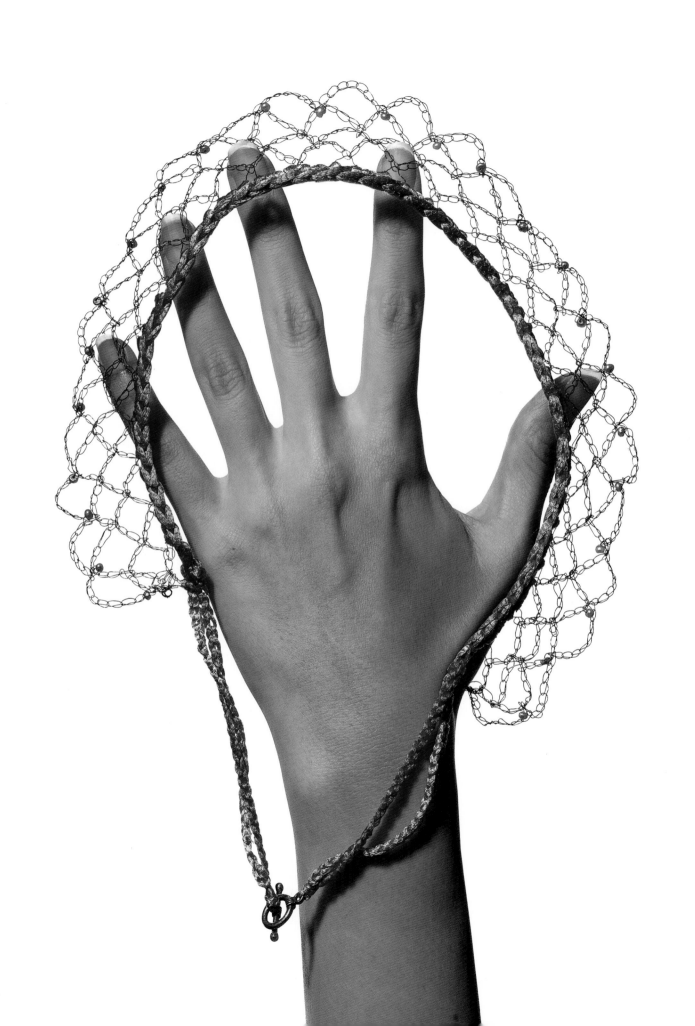

SKILL LEVEL
C 2 Easy

SIZE
S (M, L)

FINISHED MEASUREMENTS
20 (22, 24)"/51 (56, 61)cm

MATERIALS
50yds (46m) fuchsia (#S15)
Artistic Wire (A), 30 gauge

15yds (14m) magenta
Artistic Wire (B), 30 gauge

30yds (27.5m) pinks (101)
Silk Ribbon 101 (C) (Art
Yarns)

30yds (27.5m) peaches
(116) Silk Ribbon 101 (D)
(Art Yarns)

22 (24, 26) white pearls,
size 2mm (Ancient Moon
Beads)

Copper toggle finding
(Blue Moon Beads)

Size E (3.5mm) and size B
(2.25mm) crochet hooks

Gauge: 5 ch = 1" (2.5cm)
using smaller hook

NOTIONS
Straight knitting needle,
darning needle

SPECIAL STITCH USED
Bc (see page 119)

crochet lace necklace

Estimated time: Bead stringing, 10 minutes; Crocheting, 45 minutes

before you begin
String all pearls onto wire B.

crochet
With larger hook and A, ch 104 (114, 124).

row 1 Change to smaller hook. Ch 3, sc into second foundation ch from hook, [ch 5, sk 4 ch, sc in next st] across to last 2 sts, ch 3, sk 1 st, sc into last st, turn—22 (24, 26) ch-lps.
row 2 Ch 1, sc into first ch-lp, [ch 5, sc into next ch-lp] across—21 (23, 25) ch-lps.
row 3 Ch 3, sc into first ch-lp, [ch 5, sc into next ch-lp] across to end of row, ch 3, sc into same lp as last sc—22 (24, 26) ch-lps.
row 4 With B, ch 3, [sl pearl onto hook, bc into next ch-lp, ch 5] across to last ch-lp, ending last rep ch 3 instead of ch 5, sl pearl to hook, bc into last ch-lp.

Weave a straight knitting needle in and out of each ch-lp in the last row, then use this firm edge to gently pull the necklace and block the lace.

NECKLACE TOP
With 1 strand each of C and D and larger hook, and leaving a 30" (76cm) tail at start of work, sc in each foundation ch at top of necklace—104 (114, 124) sts. Fasten off, leaving a 30" (76cm) tail at end of work.

TIES
Starting as close to edge of necklace as possible, ch 25 with tail of C. Rep for rem tail of C. Rep for each tail of D, but only work 20 ch. This creates ties to go around the back of the neck in both colors, one slightly longer than the other. Try the necklace on to see how long you'd like the ties to go and inc or dec the number of ch sts as needed. Fasten off all ties.

finishing
Sl one part of toggle finding onto one C tail and tie a small knot with matching D tail. Use darning needle to weave tails into their respective chain ties, working loose end well into chain.

CHAPTER 2 BRACELETS

A bracelet is a wonderful canvas on which to show off beads, techniques, and special touches that you've picked up in your travels. Bracelets can be as thin and simple as a chain of fine wire joined together with no closure to be worn as a bangle, or as complex as a wide cuff encrusted with a variety of beads and buttons.

rhinestone stud bangle

Estimated time: Bead stringing, 10 minutes; Knitting, 45 minutes

SKILL LEVEL
K 1 Beginner

SIZE
One size

FINISHED MEASUREMENTS
Approx 8" (20.5cm)
circumference

MATERIALS
15yds (14m) silver Artistic
Wire, 26 gauge

36 (40, 44) silver rhinestone
& pearlized stud buttons

Size 9 (5.5mm) and size 8
(5mm) knitting needles

before you begin

String all studs onto wire.

knit

With larger needles and using any CO method, [CO 1 st, sl 1 stud onto needle] 18 (20, 22) times, CO 1 st—19 (21, 23) sts, 18 (20, 22) studs.

row 1 Change to smaller needles. [K1, sl 1 stud onto needle] across to last st, k1.
row 2 Purl.
row 3 Knit.
row 4 Purl.
row 5 Knit.
Block on the needle.

Using any method, BO all sts loosely.

finishing

Roll last 4 rows up so the studs in the first 2 rows sit to the outside. Join ends of the bangle by "sewing" with a loose end of wire. Twist, coil, and crimp loose wire ends to inside of bangle.

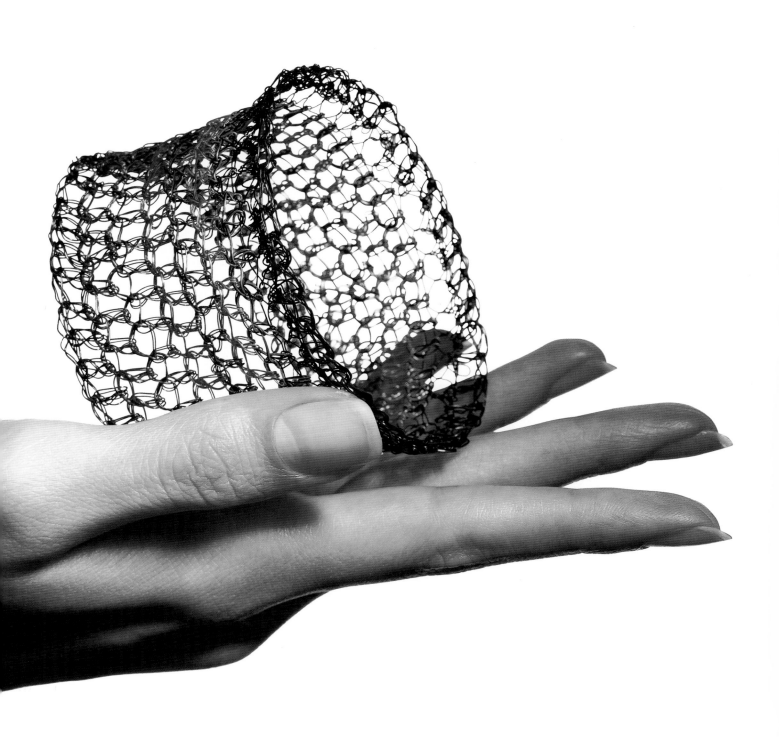

SKILL LEVEL
C 2 Easy

SIZE
S (M, L)

FINISHED MEASUREMENTS
6 (7, 8)"/15 (18, 20.5)cm circumference

MATERIALS
15yds (14m) lemon (#S12) Artistic Wire (A), 30 gauge

15yds (14m) tangerine (#S11) Artistic Wire (B), 30 gauge

15yds (14m) fuchsia (#S15) Artistic Wire (C), 30 gauge

30yds (27.5m) orchid (#S07) Artistic Wire (D), 30 gauge

60yds (55m) black (#02) Artistic Wire (E), 30 gauge

SPECIAL STITCH USED
Hdc (see page 119)

crochet rainbow cuff

Estimated time: Crocheting, 1½ hours

crochet

With E, loosely ch 30 (35, 40) sts; join with a sl st to form ring.

rnd 1 Ch 1, holding 1 strand of A tog with 1 strand of E, hdc in each st around, join with a sl st—30 (35, 40) sts. Drop E, allowing it to rest to the inside (WS) of the cuff.

rnd 2 Ch 1, holding 1 strand of B tog with the strand of A, hdc in each st around, join with a sl st. Break A.

rnd 3 Ch 1, holding the strand of E tog with the strand of B, hdc in each st around, join with a sl st. Drop E, allowing it to rest to the inside (WS) of the cuff.

rnd 4 Ch 1, holding 1 strand of C tog with the strand of B, hdc in each st around, join with a sl st. Break B.

rnd 5 Ch 1, holding the strand of E tog with the strand of C, hdc in each st around, join with a sl st. Drop E, allowing it to rest to the inside (WS) of the cuff.

rnd 6 Ch 1, holding 1 strand of D tog with the strand of C, hdc in each st around, join with a sl st. Break C.

rnd 7 Ch 1, holding the strand of E tog with the strand of D, hdc in each st around, join with a sl st. Break both strands, leaving a 5" (12.5cm) tail.

finishing

With 1 strand each of D and E held tog, working around foundation ch into bottom of rnd 1, hdc in each st around, join with a sl st. Break wires, leaving a 5" (12.5cm) tail. Twist, coil, and crimp loose wires to inside (WS) of cuff. Block cuff by placing both left and right index fingers into the cuff so the fingers are pointing at each other, then rotating cuff steadily to even out sts.

mahjong tile bracelet

Estimated time: Bead stringing, 1 hour; Knitting, 2 hours

before you begin

Create 7 double lp tiles, but do not prestring on wire; they will be attached as the piece is knit. String all seed beads onto wire A.

knit

With larger needles and 1 strand each of A and C held tog, using the long-tail method and leaving a 12" (30.5cm) tail of C, CO 27 (29, 31) sts.

row 1 (WS) Change to smaller needles. Knit.

rows 2 & 14 (RS) [P1, sl bead onto needle and hold in place with right hand as you work the next st] across to last st, p1—26 (28, 30) beads.

rows 3, 5, 7, 9, & 11 Using the fiber(s) used in prev row, knit.

row 4 Drop C (do not cut) and with A only, p1 (2, 3), sl top circle of tile onto lp of next st, sl st onto right-hand needle, [p3, sl top circle of tile onto lp of next st, sl st onto right-hand needle] 6 times, p1 (2, 3). NOTE: The tiles will be hanging off the work until the other end is attached on row 13.

rows 6 & 10 With A and C, purl.

rows 8 & 12 With A only, purl.

row 13 With A only, k1 (2, 3), sl bottom circle of tile onto lp of next st, sl st onto right-hand needle, [k3, sl bottom circle of tile onto lp of next st, sl st onto right-hand needle] 6 times, k1 (2, 3).

rows 15 & 16 Work in St st as established.

Block on the needle.

Work slipped BO across work, leaving a 5" (12.5cm) tail of A and a 12" (30.5cm) tail of C.

finishing

Sew 3 hooks to one edge of cuff. Sew 3 "bar" eyes to matching opposite edge of cuff.

SKILL LEVEL
K 3 Intermediate

SIZE
S (M, L)

FINISHED MEASUREMENTS
6 (7, 8)"/15 (18, 20.5)cm

MATERIALS:
100yds (91.5m) goldtone Artistic Wire (A), 26 gauge

15yds (14m) red Artistic Wire (B), 22 gauge

100yds (91.5m) red/orange/yellow Silk Ribbon 101 (C) (Artyarns)

52 (56, 60) silver-lined red glass seed beads, size 6/0 (Ambrosia Arts)

7 mahjong tile beads, size ⅝" x 1" (1.5 x 2.5cm) (Ancient Moon Beads)

Hook-and-bar eyes

Size 6 (4mm) and size 3 (3.25mm) knitting needles

Size F (3.75mm) crochet hook (optional, for BO)

SPECIAL STITCHES USED
Double lp tile (see page 119), LTCO (see page 93–94), slipped BO (see page 120)

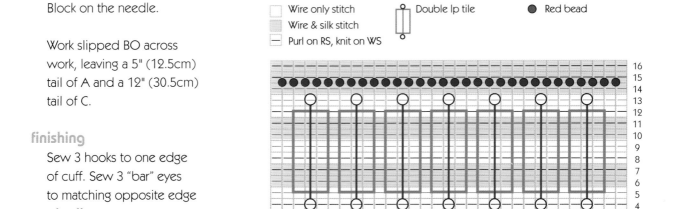

☐ Wire only stitch
▨ Wire & silk stitch
— Purl on RS, knit on WS
⃝ Double lp tile
● Red bead

crocheted pearl &
tangerine bangle

Estimated time: Bead stringing, 30 minutes; Crocheting, 1 hour

before you begin

String all pearls onto wire.

crochet

With larger hook, [ch 1, sl bead onto hook] 28 (31, 34) times, join with a sl st in first st to form ring.

rnd 1 Change to smaller hook. Work around each pearl by placing hook under bracelet and pulling up a lp, then placing hook over bracelet and pulling another lp through 2 lps on hook (sc made). Rep around entire bracelet.

rnd 2 Rep rnd 1. It may be necessary to twist the pearls a bit to pull them to the outside of the bangle. Fasten off. Cut wire, leaving a 5" (12.5cm) tail. Twist, coil, and crimp loose ends of wire to inside of bangle.

SKILL LEVEL
C 3 Intermediate

SIZE
S (M, L)

FINISHED MEASUREMENTS
6 (7, 8)"/15 (18, 20.5)cm
circumference

MATERIALS
30yds (27.5m) tangerine
(#S11) Artistic Wire, 28
gauge

28 (31, 34) white rice pearls,
size 4mm (The Bead Hut)

Size G (4mm) and size F
(3.75mm) crochet hooks

CHAPTER 3 SETS

Mixing several pieces of jewelry with the same bead family or wire color can make a powerful fashion statement. Any of these sets can be worked up individually, but I feel they complement each other quite beautifully and a set would make an exceptional gift. When working two pieces that are to be worn together, be sure to purchase enough of the materials to make both pieces, and match finishing techniques as closely as possible to lend a uniform feeling to the set.

blue velvet pearl choker

Estimated time: Bead stringing, 45 minutes; Knitting, 1½ minutes
see page 48

see page 48

before you begin

String all beads on the wire in the foll manner: hold ¼ of each of the seed beads and smaller dk gray pearls along with 8 of the lt gray pearls in your hand. String them randomly until there are approx 51 beads on the wire. Add another ¼ of each type of bead to your hand and string these beads randomly until there are approx 100 beads on the wire. Rep this process, gradually using up the smaller beads and ending by stringing mostly 8mm and 6mm beads. (When you look at the wire, the beads should roughly graduate in size from larger to smaller as you look from the end of the wire to the spool (see page 102).

knit

With larger needles and wire, [CO 1 st, sl 1 bead onto needle] 32 times.

row 1 (WS) Change to smaller needles. [K1, sl 1 bead onto needle] across.

row 2 (RS) [P1, sl 1 bead onto needle] across.

Rep last 2 rows 2 more times for a total of 6 rows, working last rep of row 2 using larger needle. There should be 7 rows of beads on the necklace, including the CO row.

BO using the pulled-lp method.

finishing

Twist, coil, and crimp the loose wire ends and flatten them against the wrong side of the choker.

Create bars at either end of piece by inserting a 12" (30.5cm) piece of wire into the first CO st and folding it in half. Twist the two halves of wire around each other until a tight double thickness of wire is formed just slightly shorter than the width of the choker. Lay this twisted piece along the edge of the choker and insert one of the wire ends into the BO st at the top of the work.

SKILL LEVEL
K 2 Easy

SIZE
One size

FINISHED MEASUREMENT
19" (48.5cm)

MATERIALS
50yds (46m) silver Artistic Wire, 26 gauge

24" (61cm) dark blue velvet ribbon, 1½" (4cm) wide

28 light blue Swarovski glass pearls, size 8mm

28 dark gray Swarovski glass pearls, size 8mm

48 light gray Swarovski glass pearls, size 6mm

60 dark gray Swarovski glass pearls, size 4mm

60 silver-lined midnight blue glass seed beads, size 6/0 (Ambrosia Arts)

Size 8 (5mm) and size 6 (4mm) knitting needles

NOTIONS
Sewing needle and thread (to match velvet), hook and eyes

SPECIAL STITCHE USED
Pulled-lp BO (see page 105)

Cont twisting the wires tog to secure the bar along the edge of the choker. Cut twisted end so that it measures ⅝" (1.5cm) from point where bar joins top of choker. Coil twisted end and crimp to wrong side of choker. Rep for other end of choker.

Hold choker to front of neck and have a friend measure the distance between ends around back of neck. Cut two pieces of velvet to this measurement. Insert one velvet ribbon under one edge bar so that the right side is showing. With right sides tog, sew ends of this ribbon tog, then gently slide ribbon so the seam is to the wrong side of the choker. Rep for the other end of the choker. Sew hook and eyes to folded edges of ribbon so choker meets at center back.

blue velvet cuff bracelet

Estimated time: Bead stringing, 45 minutes; Knitting, 1½ hours
see page 49

before you begin

String all beads on the wire in a random manner, working a few more of the larger beads at the start and end of the stringing process than in the middle.

knit

With larger needles and wire, [CO 1 st, sl 1 bead onto needle] 28 times.

row 1 (WS) Change to smaller needles. [K1, sl 1 bead onto needle] across.

row 2 (RS) [P1, sl 1 bead onto needle] across.

row 3 Knit.

row 4 Purl.

row 5 Work YYK in each st as foll: [K1, wrapping wire twice around needle] across, being sure to work loosely. There will be 2 lps for each st on the needle (56 lps total).

row 6 Purl 1 lp of each st, allowing second lp to drop off needle—28 sts.

rows 7 & 8 Rep rows 3 & 4.

rows 9 & 10 Rep rows 1 & 2.

row 11 Change to larger needles. [K1, sl 1 bead onto needle] across. Block piece on the needle, pulling tightly to open up the double wraps in row 5.

BO using the pulled-lp method.

finishing

Hand-block piece so that sts are even. Using one of the ends of wire, "sew" the edges of the cuff bracelet tog. Twist, coil, and crimp the loose wire ends and flatten them against the wrong side of the cuff.

SIZE
One size

FINISHED MEASUREMENTS
Circumference approx 8" (20cm) expanded, 6" (15 cm) compressed.
Height approx 3½" (7cm)

MATERIALS
50yds (46m) silver Artistic Wire, 26 gauge

12" (30.5cm) dark blue velvet ribbon, ¾" (19mm) wide

30 light blue Swarovski glass pearls, size 8mm

30 dark gray Swarovski glass pearls, size 8mm

30 light gray Swarovski glass pearls, size 6mm

30 dark gray Swarovski glass pearls, size 4mm

48 silver-lined midnight blue glass seed beads, size 6/0 (Ambrosia Arts)

Size 8 (5mm) and size 6 (4mm) knitting needles

NOTIONS
Sewing needle and thread (to match velvet)

SPECIAL STITCHES USED
Pulled-lp BO (see page 105), YYK (see page 120)

Gently pull the cuff wide and sl over the hand. Holding the top of the cuff against the palm with the middle finger, tug gently at the bottom with the other hand; turn and rep all around the cuff. This will gently lengthen the cuff and bring it in for a tighter fit around the wrist.

When cuff is sized correctly for your wrist, weave a piece of velvet between the double wraps in row 5, bringing both ends tog at seam and tying in a knot. Be sure cuff isn't too tight to fit over your hand when the ribbon is tied! Clip the ends of the ribbon in double points, and tack in place over the wire seam.

Wearing knit wire cuffs is a blast, but figuring out how to put them on can be a bit of a mystery. Before donning the cuff, insert both pointer fingers into the cuff and expand it as fully as possible. Then slip the cuff over your hand, holding the top edge between the heel of your palm and fingertips, and pull the bottom edge with your free hand. Rotate the cuff a bit and pull again. Repeat this procedure all the way around the cuff, being careful not to pull too hard to any one point, until you have the desired fit.

copper & silver lace band necklace

Estimated time: Bead stringing, 30 minutes; Knitting, 1 hour
see page 54

before you begin

Holding 1 strand each of A and B tog, string 96+ beads in the foll manner: [string 2 copper beads, string 2 pink beads] at least 24 times. If you want a longer necklace, you may want to string more beads. It may be helpful to twist the ends of the wire tog to make a firmer end to sl through the beads.

knit

Holding 1 strand each of A and B tog, and using as one strand throughout, CO 9 sts.
row 1 (RS) Sl bead onto needle, k1, p1, k2tog-R, yo, k1, yo, k2tog-L, p1, k1, sl bead onto needle.
rows 2 & 4 (WS) K2, p5, k2.
row 3 Sl bead onto needle, k1, p1, k1, k2tog-R, yo, k2, p1, k1, sl bead onto needle.

Rep rows 1–4 until piece is desired length. Every 5–10 rows, block piece on needle by gently pulling lengthwise, then widthwise, several times to even out the sts. Pull against the firmness of the needle to aid in this process. When piece is desired length, BO all sts.

finishing

Weave CO and BO tails through sts at each end of piece and draw up to slightly gather the ends of the piece. Use the tails to "sew" a toggle and ring onto the ends of the pieces. Wrap the wire around the ends of the piece. Twist, coil, and crimp the loose wire ends and flatten them against the wrong side of the necklace.

SKILL LEVEL
K 3 Intermediate

SIZE
One Size

FINISHED MEASUREMENTS
Make this piece as long or short as you desire

MATERIALS
100yds (91.5m) copper Artistic Wire (A), 30 gauge

100yds (91.5m) silver Artistic Wire (B), 30 gauge

48+ copper rondele beads, size 6mm (Multi Creations NJ, Inc.)

48+ silver-lined pink glass seed beads, size 6/0 (Ambrosia Arts)

Copper toggle finding (Multi Creations NJ, Inc.)

Size 4 (3.5mm) knitting needles

SPECIAL STITCHES USED
K2tog-L (see page 101), K2tog-R (see page 101), yo (see page 100)

SKILL LEVEL
K 3 Intermediate

SIZE
One Size

FINISHED MEASUREMENTS
Varies

MATERIALS
50yds (46m) copper Artistic Wire (A), 30 gauge

50yds (46m) silver Artistic Wire (B), 30 gauge

24+ silver-lined pink glass seed beads, size 6/0 (Ambrosia Arts)

24+ copper rondele beads, size 6mm (Multi Creations NJ, Inc.)

Copper hook-and-eye finding (Multi Creations NJ, Inc.)

Size 4 (3.5mm) knitting needles

SPECIAL STITCHES USED
K2tog-L (see page 101), k2tog-R (see page 101), yo (see page 100)

copper & silver lace bracelet

Estimated time: Bead stringing, 30 minutes; Knitting, 45 minutes
see page 55

before you begin

Holding 1 strand each of A and B tog, string 48+ beads in the foll manner: [string 2 copper beads, string 2 pink beads] at least 12 times. If you want a longer bracelet, you may want to string more beads. It may be helpful to twist the ends of the wire tog to make a firmer end to sl through the beads.

Work and finish as for Copper & Silver Lace Band Necklace, working to desired bracelet length.

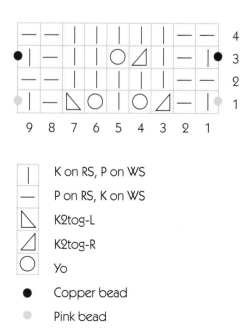

	K on RS, P on WS
—	P on RS, K on WS
◺	K2tog-L
◿	K2tog-R
○	Yo
●	Copper bead
⬤	Pink bead

copper dangle potato pearl necklace

Estimated time: Bead stringing, 2 hours; Knitting, 1 hour
see page 58

before you begin

Make 13 square dangles.

Square dangle: Use the flat edge of a pair of pliers to coil the end of a 3½" (9cm) piece of wire B. Press the coil tightly to harden it. Sl 1 seed bead, 1 square bead, then 2 seed beads onto the wire. Coil the top of the wire to create a hanging lp. Crimp flat to harden the lp.

String beads onto wire A in the foll order: 13 rice pearls, 41 seed beads, [1 seed bead, 1 potato pearl, 1 seed bead, 1 dangle] 13 times, 1 seed bead, 1 potato pearl, 1 seed bead.

knit

With larger needles, A, and using the Long Tail method, CO 56 sts in the foll manner: CO 1 st, [sl 1 bead onto needle, CO 1 st] 55 times.

row 1 (WS) Change to smaller needles. P2, [sl bead onto needle, p2] across—27 seed beads.
row 2 (RS) K2, [sl beads onto needle, k4] across to last 2 sts, sl bead onto needle, k2—14 seed beads.
row 3 (WS) P4, [sl rice pearl onto needle, p4] across—13 rice pearls. Block on the needle. Bind off as foll: [BO 1 st, (sl next bead onto needle, BO 1 st) 3 times] rep 13 times. Cut wire, leaving a 6" tail and pull through last st.

finishing

Do not BO Sts! Sl silk cord through the sts on the needle. The necklace may be tied around the neck, or a hook-and-loop finding can be attached at the appropriate place on the cord and the extra cord can be cut away.

SKILL LEVEL
K 3 Intermediate

SIZE
Adjustable

FINISHED MEASUREMENTS
Varies

MATERIALS
50yds (46m) copper Artistic Wire (A), 28 gauge

2yds (2m) copper Artistic Wire (B), 22 gauge

24" (61cm) olive green silk cord (Mokuba)

13 green square stone beads, size 4mm (Blue Moon Beads)

108 silver-lined gold glass seed beads, size 6/0 (Ambrosia Arts)

13 white rice pearls, size 4mm (The Bead Hut)

14 olive potato pearls, size 6mm (The Bead Hut)

Copper toggle finding (Multi Creations NJ, Inc.)

Size 6 (4mm) and size 4 (3.5mm) knitting needles

NOTIONS
Sewing thread (to match silk cord), sewing needle, hook-and-loop finding (optional)

SPECIAL STITCHES USED
Long tail CO (see page 101), non-bind-off BO (see page 105), square dangle (see page 120)

SKILL LEVEL
3 Intermediate

SIZE
One Size

FINISHED MEASUREMENT
8" (20.5cm)

MATERIALS
50yds (46m) copper Artistic Wire, 28 gauge

24" (61cm) olive green silk cord (Mokuba)

130 silver-lined gold glass seed beads, size 6/0 (Ambrosia Arts)

17 white rice pearls, size 4mm (The Bead Hut)

26 olive potato pearls, size 6mm (The Bead Hut)

Copper toggle finding (Multi Creations NJ, Inc.)

Size 6 (4mm) and size 4 (3.5mm) knitting needles

SPECIAL STITCHES USED
Long-tail CO (see page 93), pulled-lp BO (see page 105)

| K on RS, P on WS

 6/0 silver-lined glass gold beads

⬭ 4mm white rice pearls

● 6mm olive potato pearls

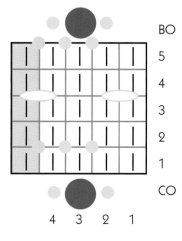

copper potato pearl bracelet

Estimated time: Bead stringing, 1 hour; Knitting, 1½ hours
see page 59

before you begin
String beads in the foll order:
[1 seed bead, 1 potato pearl, 1 seed bead] 13 times, 39 seed beads, 17 rice pearls, 39 seed beads, [1 seed bead, 1 potato pearl, 1 seed bead] 13 times.

knit
Using the long-tail method and with larger needle, [CO 1 st, (sl next bead onto needle, CO 1 st) 3 times] 13 times, CO 1 st—53 sts, 13 sets of (seed bead/potato pearl/seed bead).

row 1 (WS) Change to smaller needles. [P1, (sl bead onto needle, p1) 3 times] across to last st, p1—39 seed beads.
row 2 (RS) Knit.
row 3 (WS) P2, [sl rice pearl onto needle, p3] across.
row 4 Knit.
row 5 With larger needle, rep row 1.

Block on the needle. BO as foll: [BO 1 st, (sl next bead onto needle, BO 1 st) 3 times] rep to last st, cut wire leaving an 8" tail and pull through the last lp.

finishing
Block piece so sts are even and bracelet fits comfortably around the wrist. Tug bracelet lengthwise slightly to create a rounded point at each end. Using the loose wire ends, secure hook-and-loop finding to either end. Twist, coil, and crimp loose wire ends to wrong side of bracelet.

granny square necklace

Estimated time: Crocheting, 45 minutes

see page 62

crochet

With larger hook and 1 strand each of A & B held tog, ch 101 (111, 121).

row 1 Change to smaller hook. With B only, hdc into second ch from hook, [ch 1, sk 1 ch, 2 hdc in next ch] across to last ch, ch 1, hdc in last ch-50 (55, 60) ch-sps.

row 2 Return to start of row and with A only, ch 5, [3 dc in ch-sp, ch 2] across to last hdc, dc in last hdc, turn.

row 3 With larger hook and both strands held tog, ch 2, [3 hdc in next ch-sp] across to last st, hdc in last st. Fasten off.

finishing

Work all wire ends to top of necklace (foundation ch) and use wire ends to attach toggle-and-loop finding to top ends of necklace.

SKILL LEVEL
C 3 Intermediate

SIZE
S (M, L)

FINISHED MEASUREMENTS
20 (22, 24)"/51 (56, 61)cm

MATERIALS
30yds (27.5m) peacock blue Artistic Wire (A), 30 gauge

30yds (27.5m) chartreuse Artistic Wire (B), 30 gauge

Silver toggle finding

Size E (3.5mm) and size B (2.25mm) crochet hooks

SPECIAL STITCHES USED
Hdc (see page 119),
dc (see page 109)

SKILL LEVEL
C 3 Intermediate

SIZE
One size

FINISHED MEASUREMENT
8" (20.5cm) long

MATERIALS
30yds (27.5m) peacock blue
Artistic Wire (A), 30 gauge

30yds (27.5m) chartreuse
Artistic Wire (B), 30 gauge

Size E (3.5mm) and size B
(2.25mm) crochet hooks

SPECIAL STITCHES USED
Hdc (see page 119),
dc (see page 109)

granny circle bangle
Estimated time: Crocheting, 2 hours
see page 63

Note: Make 2 small medallions and 1 large medallion. Changes for large appear in parentheses.

crochet
With A & B held tog and larger hook, ch 6, join with a sl st in first ch to form a ring.

rnd 1 Ch 1, 12 sc (hdc) into ring, join with sl st to first sc (hdc).

rnd 2 With smaller hook and B only, ch 3, dc in same st, ch 1, [2 dc in next st, ch 1] around, join with sl st to top of beg ch—12 ch-sps.

rnd 3 With A, ch 2, 2 hdc in next ch-sp, ch 1, [3 hdc in next ch-sp, ch 1] around, join with sl st to top of beg ch.

rnd 4 With A & B held tog and larger hook, 3 hdc in each ch-sp around—36 hdc. Fasten off.

finishing
Use the loose wire ends to join medallions tog. Place one smaller medallion on either side of larger medallion. Twist, coil, and crimp against wrong side of medallions. Bangle can be slightly stretched to fit over hand and will hang loose off the wrist. If a tighter fit is desired, add a toggle-and-loop finding between first and last medallions instead of attaching them with wire ends.

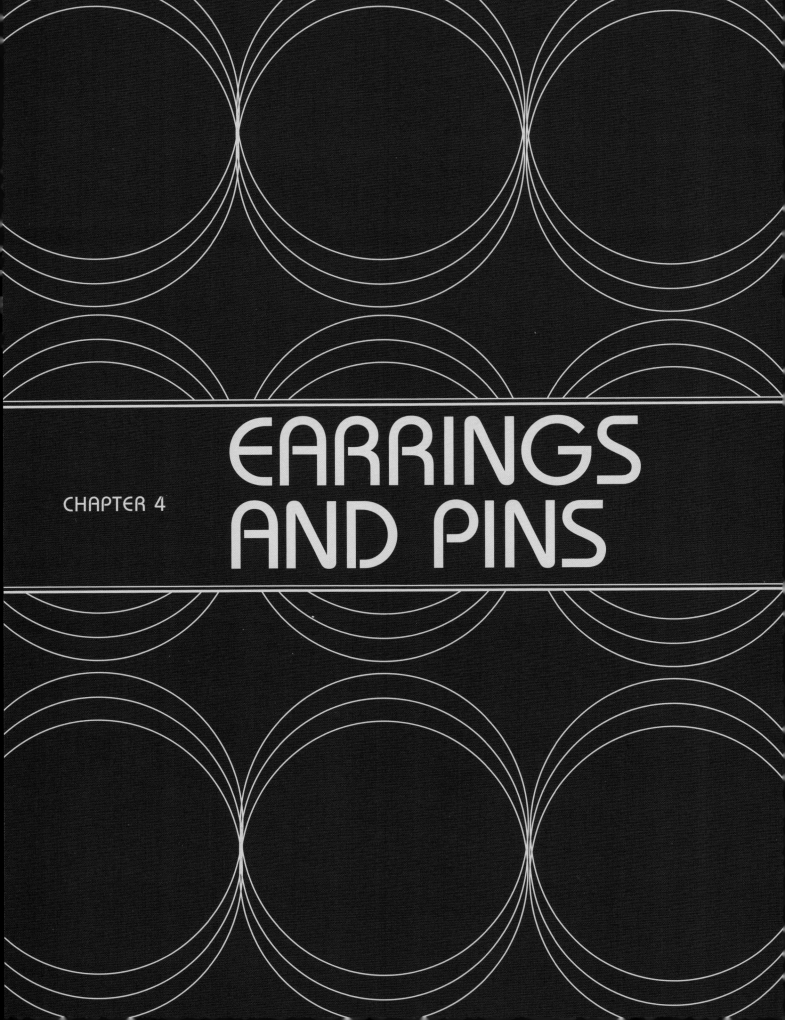

CHAPTER 4

EARRINGS AND PINS

Perhaps the easiest and most comfortable jewelry to wear, pins and earrings may be quite small or rather large—but they always take center stage! When giving these items as gifts, it's important to match the personality of the recipient with the size of the piece. Sometimes the smallest piece achieves the most dramatic effect.

wreath earrings

Estimated time: Knitting, 45 minutes each

NOTE: The right (public) side of this piece is the reverse stockinette st side (purl side) of the work.

knit

With larger needles and A, CO 24 sts.

row 1 (RS) Change to smaller needles. Purl.

row 2 (WS) Knit.

Block piece on the needle.

Work slipped BO across work, leaving a 5" (12.5cm) tail of wire.

finishing

Allow piece to roll onto itself so the rev St st side is facing out. If necessary, roll fabric between hands to create a wire "worm." Sew CO and BO edges tog using wire tail as thread (and a darning needle, if desired). Form into a hoop and use wire tail to join.

With B, create jump rings by coiling the wire around the larger knitting needle several times. Sl the coil off the needle and, holding the earring over a piece of light-colored paper, use your wire cutters to snip a straight line from the first coil to the last. The jump rings will fall to the paper along with extra bits of wire from the first and last coil.

Use 1 jump ring to connect the tip of the hoop to the loop on the earring hook, tightening the ring with pliers after the hoop is joined.

SKILL LEVEL
K 1 Beginner

SIZE
One size

FINISHED MEASUREMENT
1¼" (3cm) diameter

MATERIALS
15yds (14m) silver Artistic Wire (A), 26 gauge

6" (15cm) silver Artistic Wire (B), 20 gauge

Silver earring hooks

Size 6 (4mm) and size 2 (2.75mm) knitting needles

SPECIAL STITCH USED
Slipped BO (see page 120)

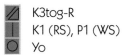

- ⊠ K3tog-R
- | K1 (RS), P1 (WS)
- ○ Yo

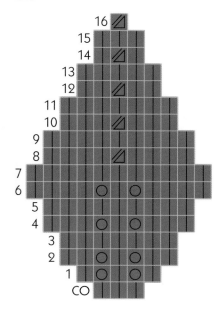

autumn leaf earrings
Estimated time: Knitting 45 minutes each

knit
LEAF (MAKE 2 IN RED, 2 IN YELLOW)
With larger needles and A or B, CO 3 sts.

row 1 Change to smaller needles. [P1, yo] twice, p1—5 sts.

row 2 K2, yo, k1, yo, k2—7 sts.

row 3 and all WS rows: Purl.

row 4 K3, yo, k1, yo, k3—9 sts.

row 6 K4, yo, k1, yo, k4—11 sts.

row 8 K4, k3tog-R, k4—9 sts.

row 10 K3, k3tog-R, k3—7 sts.

row 12 K2, k3tog-R, k2—5 sts.

row 14 K1, k3tog-R, k1—3 sts.

row 16 K3tog-R. Fasten off last st.

finishing
With C, create jump rings by coiling the wire around a size 7 knitting needle several times. Sl the coil off the needle and, holding it over a piece of light-colored paper, use your wire cutters to snip a straight line from the first coil to the last. The jump rings will fall to the paper along with extra bits of wire from the first and last coil.

Use 1 jump ring to connect the CO edge of each yellow leaf to the ring of a copper earring hook, tightening the ring with pliers after the leaves are joined. Use another jump ring to attach the CO edge of each red leaf to the center of a yellow leaf, about ⅓ of the way down from the earring hook.

crocheted leaf earrings

Estimated time: Crocheting, 30 minutes each

SKILL LEVEL
C 2 Easy

SIZE
One size

FINISHED MEASUREMENTS
1" x 1³/₄" (2.5 x 4.5cm) leaf

MATERIALS
15yds (14m) tangerine (#S11) Artistic Wire (A), 30 gauge

5yds (4.5m) tangerine Artistic Wire (B), 22 gauge

Copper earring hooks (Multi Creations NJ, Inc.)

Size C (2.75mm) crochet hook

SPECIAL STITCHES USED
Hdc (see page 119), sl st (see page 120)

before you begin

With A, loosely ch 4.

crochet

row 1 2 sc in second ch from hook and in each ch across, turn—6 sts.

row 2 Ch 1, 2 sc in first st, sc in next 4 sts, 2 sc in last st, turn—8 sts.

row 3 Ch 2, hdc in each st across, turn.

row 4 Ch 1, sc2tog, sc in next 4 sts, sc2tog, turn—6 sts.

row 5 Ch 1, sc in first 2 sts, sc2tog, sc in next 2 sts, turn—5 sts.

row 6 Ch 1, sc in first 2 sts, sc2tog, sc in last st, turn—4 sts.

row 7 Ch 1, sc in first st, sc2tog, sc in last st, turn—3 sts.

row 8 Ch 1, sc in first st, sc2tog, turn—2 sts.

row 9 Ch 1, sc2tog, turn—1 st.

row 10 Ch 2.

finishing

Sl st along edge of leaf to foundation ch. Fasten off, leaving a 5" (12.5cm) tail. Twist, coil, and crimp wire to finish. Block leaf to shape it to desired form. With B, create 2 jump rings according to the finishing instructions on page 66. Use these to attach leaf to earring hook.

◯	Ch1
8	Ch2
◖	Sl 1 st
X	Sc
✕	Sc2tog
T	Hdc

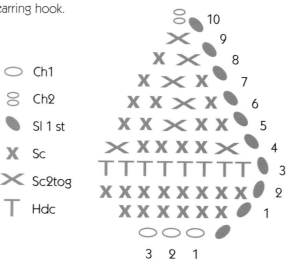

SKILL LEVEL
C 1 Beginner

SIZE
One size

FINISHED MEASUREMENT
Approx 3¹/₂" (9cm) long

MATERIALS
5yds (4.5m) purple Artistic
Wire (A), 26 gauge

12" (30.5cm) natural (#10)
Artistic Wire (B), 20 gauge

12 silver-lined gold glass
seed beads, size 6/0
(Ambrosia Arts)

12 coconut ¹/₂-round shell
beads, size 10mm
(The Bead Hut)

6 olive top-drilled pearls,
size 6mm (The Bead Hut)

4 cream pearls, size 6mm
(The Bead Hut)

Copper earring hooks
(Multi Creations NJ, Inc.)

Size D (3.25mm) crochet
hook

pearl & coconut earrings

Estimated time: Bead stringing, 15 minutes each;
Crocheting, 15 minutes each

before you begin

On wire A, string beads as foll: [2 seed beads, 1 cream pearl] twice,
2 seed beads, 6 coconut shell beads, 3 olive pearls. Rep for second
earring.

crochet

With A, ch 1, sl pearl onto hook, ch 1, sl pearl onto hook, draw wire
between 2 pearls already worked, sl pearl onto hook, ch 1, open
lp on hook wide and bring wire spool through loop, tighten to finish
off this section of earring. Sl 6 shell beads so they sit atop the
3 olive pearls, resting on the small knot you've just created. Move to
the top of the 6 shell beads and create a loose slip knot in the wire,
gently sliding it as close as possible to the top of the shell beads.

Ch 1, [sl 2 seed beads onto hook, ch 1, sl 1 cream pearl onto hook,
ch 1] twice, sl last 2 seed beads onto hook, ch 1. Break wire, leaving
an 8" (20.5cm) tail, and draw through last lp. Twist, coil, and crimp
wire tail and sl through second seed bead from top to tidy wire.

finishing

With B, create 2 jump rings according to the finishing instructions on
page 66. Sl jump ring through top seed bead and through loop on
earring hook. Close with pliers.

chain flower pin

Estimated time: Bead stringing, 10 minutes; Crochetingr; Assembly, 20 minutes
see page 76

see page 76

before you begin

String 18 beads onto the contrasting center wire color for each flower: pink beads on amethyst (D) wire, lime beads on yellow (B) wire, orange beads on yellow (B) wire.

crochet

With A, [ch 18, join with sl st in first ch to form ring] 6 times, each time slipping into the same starting st to create 6 lp petals joined by one single st. Fasten off, leaving a 6" (15cm) tail. Pull both tails through the center st toward the back of the work.

BEADED FLOWER CENTER

With B (prestrung with 18 beads), sl st into center st. [Starting in the center of petal 1, place hook under ch edges of petals 1 & 2 and pull up a lp under chains. Pass hook over ch edges of petals 1 & 2 and draw a lp through 2 lps on hook—1 sc made. (Sl bead to hook, ch 1) 3 times] around for each point where petals meet, join with a sl st to beg sc—6 sc, 18 ch and 18 beads.

finishing

Fasten off last st and break wire, leaving a 9" (23cm) tail. Push beaded flower center toward the middle of the flower and, using the tail as a sewing needle, "stitch" the beaded chains in place, securing them to the center of the flower. End by pulling tails to wrong side of flower. Twist strands tog, but do not crimp or coil.

Rep above process using wires C & D for another flower, and wires E & B for a third flower.

SKILL LEVEL
C 3 Intermediate

SIZE
One size

FINISHED MEASUREMENTS
Approx 3" (7.5cm) diameter

MATERIALS
15yds (14m) tangerine (#S11) Artistic Wire (A), 30 gauge

10yds (9m) lemon (#S12) Artistic Wire (B), 30 gauge

15yds (14m) orchid (#S07) Artistic Wire (C), 30 gauge

5yds (4.5m) amethyst (#S18) Artistic Wire (D), 30 gauge

15yds (14m) red Artistic Wire (E), 30 gauge

30yds (27.5m) sea foam green (#S09) Artistic Wire (F), 30 gauge

15yds (14m) Christmas green (#S13) Artistic Wire (G), 30 gauge

18 silver-lined pink seed beads, size 6/0

18 lime green seed beads, size 10

18 orange bugle beads, size 4mm

Size C (2.75mm) crochet hook

NOTIONS
Gold pin backing, darning needle

SPECIAL STITCHES USED
Hdc (see page 119), sl st (see page 120)

LEAVES

Work leaves as for Crocheted Leaf Earrings (page 70), working 2 leaves with F and 1 leaf with G.

Arrange leaves and twist all loose leaf wire ends. Arrange flowers on leaves and twist all flower wire groups tog under leaves. Create two coils of the twisted wires (one flower wire coil and one leaf wire coil). Crimp to wrong side of leaf to finish.

finishing

Thread an 18" (45.5cm) piece of F onto darning needle and, leaving a 5" (12.5cm) tail, "sew" flower and leaf piece onto pin backing, being careful not to involve wire in spring closure. Finish near starting point, twist starting and finishing tails tog, then coil and crimp to underside of leaf to finish.

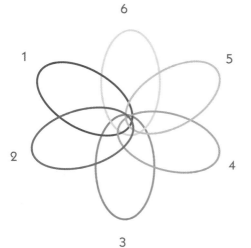

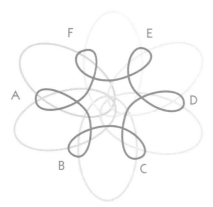

rose pin

Estimated time: Knitting, 2 hours; Assembly, 20 minutes
see page 77

ROSE PETAL (MAKE 2)

knit

Holding 1 strand each of A and B tog, with larger needles, and using the wire method, CO 60 sts.
next row Change to smaller needles. Purl.

Start Short **row** Shaping
next row K50, W&T.
next row P40, W&T.
next row K30, W&T.
next row P20, W&T.
next row K10, W&T.
next row Purl to end of row.
next row With larger needle, knit. Sl sts back onto smaller needle and work the pulled-lp BO.

LEAF (MAKE 2)

knit

Holding 1 strand each of C and D tog, with larger needles, and using the wire method, CO 3 sts.
Work leaf as for Autumn Leaf Earrings (see page 68).

finishing

Hand-block petals and leaves by pulling into desired shape firmly and gently.

Leaving loose wire ends in place to help with final finishing, curl one petal into a loose coil to resemble a rose and "sew" in place at the bottom with a strand of wire. Coil the second petal around the first,

SIZE
One size

FINISHED MEASUREMENT
Approx 3" (7.5cm) diameter, excluding leaves

MATERIALS
30yds (27.5m) fuchsia (#S15) Artistic Wire (A), 30 gauge

15yds (14m) tangerine (#S11) Artistic Wire (B), 30 gauge

15yds (14m) lemon (#S12) Artistic Wire (C), 30 gauge

15yds (14m) chartreuse (#S17) Artistic Wire (D), 30 gauge

Size 4 (3.5mm) and size 2 (2.75mm) knitting needles

NOTION
Gold pin backing

SPECIAL STITCHES USED
K3tog-L (page 103),
Yo (page 100),
W&T (page 120),
WCO (page 94)

allowing the end of the petal to rest inside the first petal coil. Sew in place at bottom. Lay the double rose on the leaves and arrange as desired. Sew leaves in place using a strand of wire. With another loose wire end, sew finished rose and leaf set to gold pin backing. Twist, coil, and crimp loose ends.

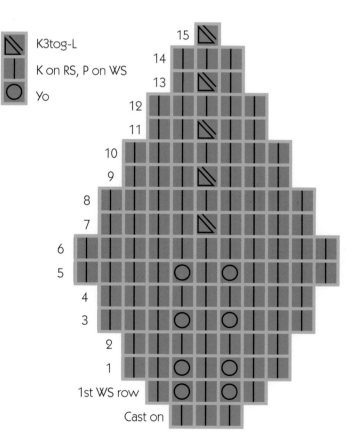

THE BASICS

Working with Wire

There are many excellent wires on the market today for craft and knitting work. The wire you choose will depend, of course, on the project.

For costume jewelry pieces, dyed copper or silver-coated dyed copper wires are best. These are easy to manipulate with knitting needles and the colors make for an interesting design element.

Dyed copper and natural copper tend to be lower priced, too, which makes them the perfect vehicle for working up ideas before investing money on high-quality fine jewelry wire to create your masterpiece.

Once you're ready to translate an idea into a piece of fine jewelry, you should invest in silver or gold wire. Fine jewelry wire comes in three basic shapes: round, half round, and square. For knitting purposes, round or half round is the best shape to use. There are also different hardness designations—my favorite is half hard. Hard wire isn't malleable enough for knitting, and dead soft can lose definition.

The best thing a new wire knitter can do, though, is work with as much wire as possible to determine her own likes and dislikes. What may work beautifully for one knitter may make another one a little crazy. Practice, have fun, and keep notes on what you have enjoyed working with.

knitting gauge

The concept of a standard knitting gauge for a wire piece, in the traditional knitters' sense of the word, is a bit ridiculous when you consider that individual wire knitting styles vary greatly. Two knitters can achieve vastly different knit wire fabric using the same gauge wire and needle size. Experimentation is the best way to determine which needle size feels best in your own hands when working with wire. In this book, suggested needle sizes are given for each piece, as are the final measurements of the piece, but these are simply benchmarks. One knitter working with a size 5 (3.75mm) needle may create a knit fabric that is looser and larger than another knitter working tightly on size 8 (5mm) needles. If you find that using a suggested needle size gives you a bracelet that is much too wide, move down a few needle sizes.

tips for working with wire spools

Wire has a mind of its own. This can be frustrating, though, when spools unwind and rolls of fine jewelry wire work themselves into an $80 mess. As with a high-spirited child, the best way to let your wire shine is to create firm but loving limits.

When working with wire on a spool, unwind several feet at a time and then hook the wire back into the slot on the spool. If there is no slot, carefully cut one. If wire unwinds from the spool like a slinky, each loop is a potential kink—and each kink is a potential breaking point. I use a small cardboard jewelry box with a slit cut into one side to hold the wire I'm currently working with. This keeps the wire from escaping and doing something we'd both regret.

When working with fine jewelry wire, which generally comes in a looped coil and looks rather like an expensive lariat, be sure to keep the coil taped closed in several places to prevent it from splaying out. Your wire will thank you for these safeguards.

When creating your piece, you may run out of wire and need to join a new spool. In that case, fold each wire end to create a check mark. Hook the checks together, and then twist the short end around the long end to lock the pieces together. Use pliers to create an even twist, and clip away any excess wire from each edge.

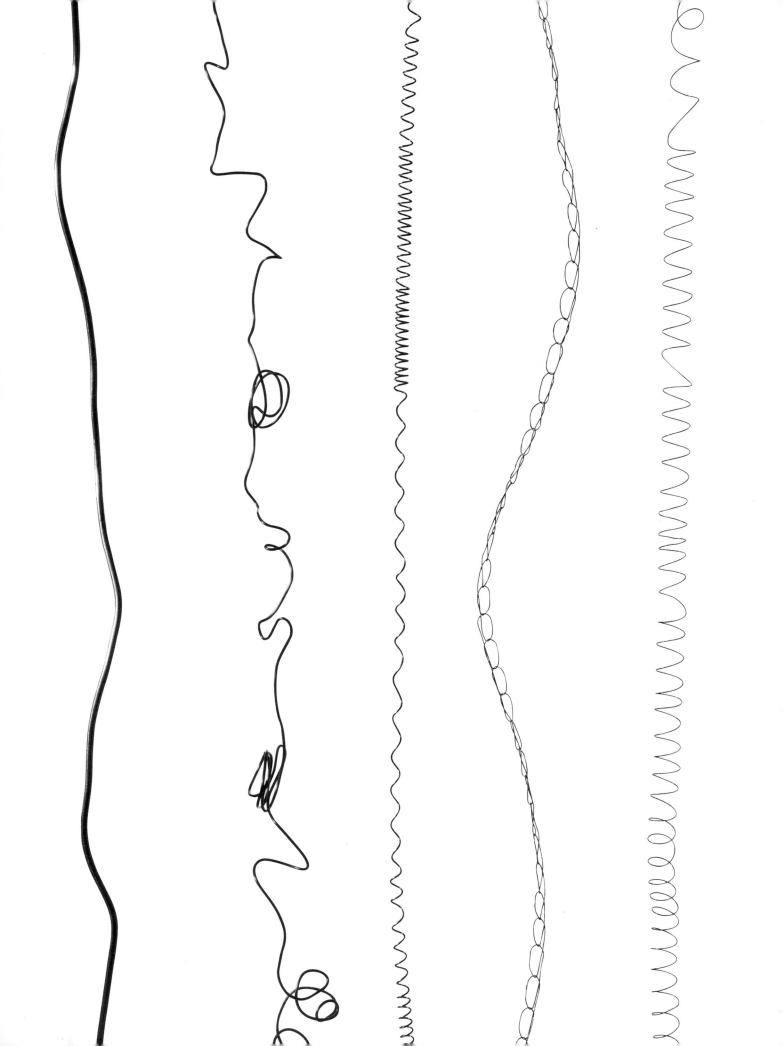

FINE JEWELRY WIRE

silver

Silver — a fine metal — is too soft in its pure form for knitting purposes. For this reason silver is generally mixed with another metal—usually copper—to provide adequate hardness. Silver that is at least 99.9% pure silver is designated as Fine Silver. Sterling Silver (92.5%), Coin Silver (90% Silver/10% Copper), and Nickel Silver (65% Copper/18% Zinc/17% Nickel) are other designations for silver in jewelry making.

gold

The number of parts per 24 that are pure gold is referred to as its karat designation. 14K gold is 14/24 pure gold, 24K gold is 24/24 (or 100%) pure gold. Anything lower than 10 karats is not legally considered gold. *Gold-filled* describes a method of bonding gold to an alloy metal and then extruding it into a specified thickness. Not to be confused with gold plate, which has much less gold content, gold-filled is of higher quality and generally contains a minimum of 10% pure gold. Gold-filled may not look as shiny as some gold-plated wire, but it will retain its coloration even when worn down. Gold-plated wire can lose the gold plate with wear.

wire gauges

In wire, gauge means an entirely different thing than it usually does in knitting. It is not a measure of the number of stitches per inch in the finished fabric, but a method of measuring the diameter of the wire. A wire's gauge is equivalent to the number of wires that can fit into a specified area. For instance, thirty-six thin wires will fit into the same space that nine thick wires would, so the gauge of the thin wire would be 36, the gauge of the thick wire, 9. Understanding this rule makes it easy to remember that a smaller gauge means a thicker piece of wire—a counterintuitive concept.

For knitting purposes, any wire between gauge 24 and 30 is relatively easy to handle. Low gauges (20, 22) may be knit, but they are rather thick and can be hard on the hands. High gauges (32, 34) are about the thickness of a human hair, and can be stranded together with other wires to add beautiful highlights or make a lovely knit fabric. Individually, these strands are wonderful for crochet work, but they tend to break too easily for knitted pieces. Even if you are able to complete a hand-knit necklace or bracelet in 34-gauge wire, the chances are good that the first time you wear it, it will break. However, if you are a machine knitter, these finer wires are perfect!

Lower-gauge wires (14, 16, 18) are excellent for making findings (hooks and eyes, toggles, clasps) for your knit jewelry pieces.

Wire is forever? Probably not. Like any hand-crafted item, wire jewelry will last longer if well-cared for. The stronger the wire, the longer the piece will remain beautiful and wearable. Pieces that require more flexibility benefit from the use of jump rings (small, hard circles of wire) to connect the varoius elements and lessen the stress on the thinner wires.

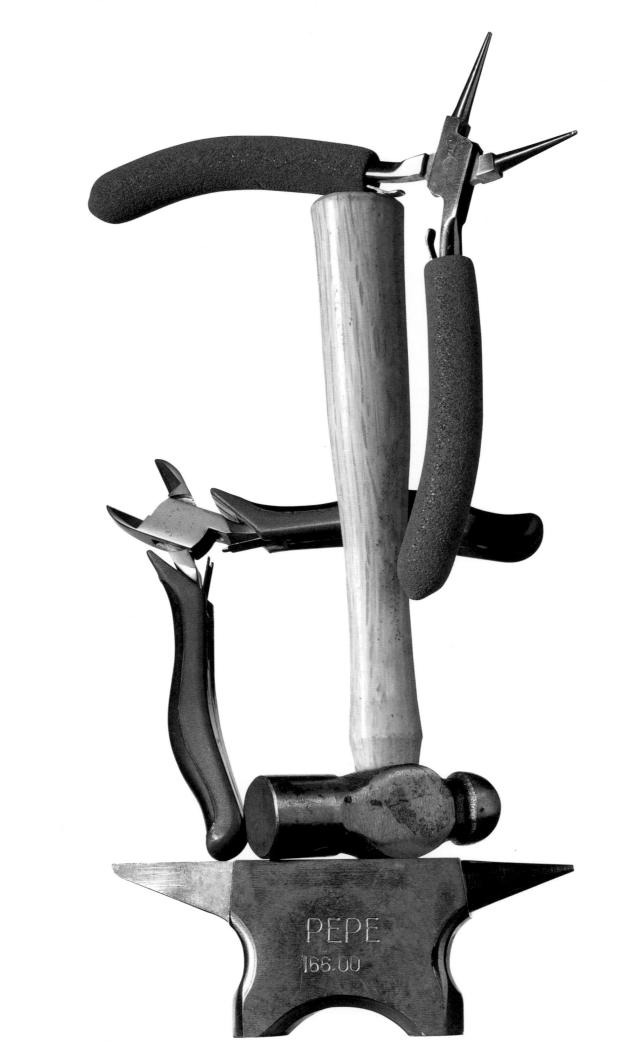

TOOLS FOR KNITTING WITH WIRE

knitting needles & crochet hooks

Expensive knitting needles and crochet hooks are fine for working with wire, but I find that cheap aluminum tools work the best (and suffer the least!). Wood needles and hooks can break and become grooved, Teflon-coated tools can become scratched, plastic or casein hooks and needles are not strong enough, and bone is too precious!

I like steel crochet hooks for working with wire, but these can sometimes scratch the finish off a coated wire. It's good to have a wide range of sizes of aluminum knitting needles and at least one crochet hook, which can be useful in grabbing dropped stitches and is necessary for some wire bind-offs. Most wire knitting projects are worked on needle sizes 4–8 U.S. (3.75–5mm).

Pliers

In addition to knitting needles, pliers and wire cutters are also very useful for manipulating the wire when finishing jewelry pieces. Here is a very basic selection:

Round-Nose Pliers have rounded prongs that are conical in shape and perfect for forming coils and spirals.

Needle-Nose Pliers have a long, pointed long nose and are excellent for grabbing and twisting wire that is hard to hold with fingers and for finishing pieces.

Chain-Nose Pliers look like shortened needle-nose pliers, but are excellent for working in smaller areas and for crimping ends.

The tool may not make the craftsperson, but it can certainly help! If possible, try a variety of tools before purchasing any to see how comfortable a particular pair of pliers or ball peen hammer is in your own hands. Many manufacturers make tools in several sizes to suit different hands. It's also best to purchase the highest quality tools you can afford—poorly made, inexpensive tools are never a bargain.

Flat-Nosed Pliers have flat, non-ridged, wide prongs and are excellent for holding a wire piece as you work.

Smoothing/Nylon/Teflon-Nose Pliers/Wire Cutters have smooth prongs that are MAGICAL in straightening out bent or twisted wire, especially higher gauges of wire. For many of the higher-gauge wires, a sturdy pair of scissors will work fine for cutting wire. However to create a beveled cut or to cut a lower-gauge wire, flush cutting tools are necessary.

Findings for all types of wire jewelry, from closures to earring hooks, are available in the beading- or jewelry-making section of your local craft shop.
top row: Bar-and-loop closure, hook closure, barrel clasp, pin backing, and earring hooks.
middle row: Earring hooks, 4-strand clasp, 3-strand clasp, large bar-and-loop closure, earring loops, and 3-strand joiners.
botton row: End pins, earring hooks, crimp-able necklace closure, and bar-and-loop closure.

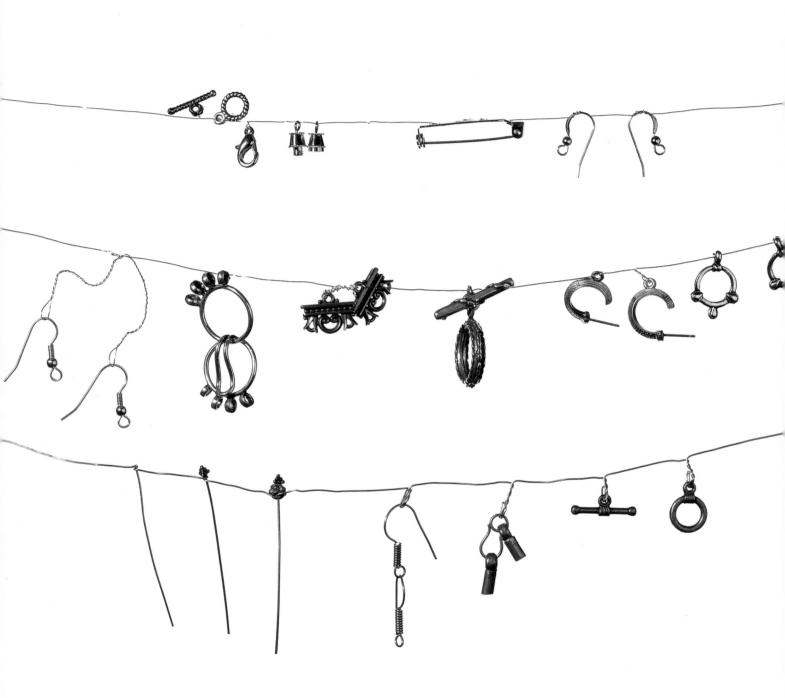

CHAPTER 5

KNITTING WITH WIRE

So much of working with a new material entails learning through practice and developing familiarity. No amount of instruction can take the place of working with the wire, getting to know the feeling of a new medium, and learning the lessons your own hands will teach you! It is vital that before you start any of the pieces in this book you take the time to cast on 8 stitches on any size needle and simply work up a small wire swatch. Use this swatch to try out new techniques and introduce your hands to the wire.

KNITTING

I find that using the Combination method of knitting makes knitting with wire much easier. A combination of the Eastern and Western methods of knitting, Combination knitting is also sometimes called Eastern Uncrossed. Creating a knit or purl stitch using the Combination method results in less wire manipulation, which leads to less bending and breaking of the wire. Of course, no matter how you knit you will be able to create lovely knit fabric.

A wire can only be bent so many times before it weakens to the point that it will break. It's important NOT to overmanipulate your wire as you knit with it. Avoid wrapping wire around your hand in a cat's cradle—it won't help with wire knitting and it adds unnecessary stress to the wire.

No matter what method you use in your knitting, it is much easier to knit with wire if you are able to hold the wire in your left hand. I suggest that you practice it for a bit with a non-wire fiber. If this feels awkward to you, take comfort in the fact that most wire knitting projects are rather small, so you won't be forced to hold your yarn in an uncomfortable manner for too terribly long. If you absolutely must knit with the yarn in your right hand, be aware of the amount of bending and twisting you are incorporating into your knitting and try to reduce it as much as possible.

Casting On

Because of the non-elastic nature of wire, many cast-on methods are not ideal for wire knitting. Some knitters prefer not to cast on at all, but rather to simply wrap the wire around the needle and use each wrap as a cast-on loop. With heavier-gauge wire, this is usually the best route, but it generally creates a rather messy start.

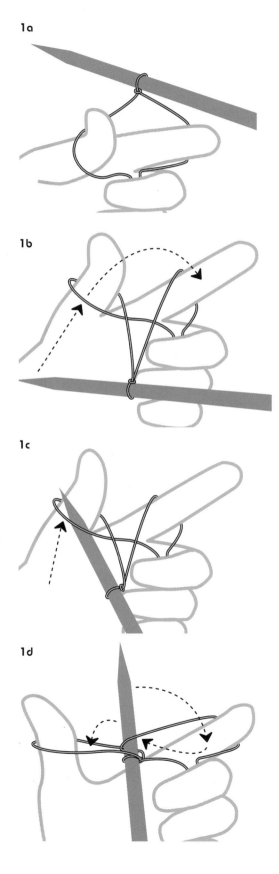

1a

1b

1c

1d

Long Tail Cast-On (LTCO)

Once the initial slip knot is fixed to the needle, any beads that are strung on the wire can be slid, one by one, onto the needle to add a lovely beaded edging. Note that this will give a rather substantial edge because you are essentially knitting the first row as you cast on. I prefer to use this method when I'm adding beads as part of the cast-on process

Preparation

The length of the tail will vary depending on how many stitches are to be cast on, but a rule of thumb is to wrap the wire around the needle as many times as there are stitches to be bound on. The length of this wrapped piece will be the tail used in the cast-on.

Alternatively, two different pieces of wire—in different colors for a tipped cast-on—can be used when casting on many stitches.

Make a slip knot in the wire at the point where the tail begins and slip this onto the needle. Be sure to keep the tail toward you and the spool to the back of the needle.

Instructions

step 1 Holding the needle in the right hand, slip your left thumb and index finger between the two strands and separate. Hold the two strands of wire securely in your left hand. **(1a)**

step 2 Spread your thumb and index finger apart and turn your palm upward. Touch the tip of the needle to the base of your thumb and slide it up under the wire. **(1b)**

step 3 Following the path of the arrows as shown, pass the needle over the strand wrapped around your index finger (1), use the tip of the needle to grab the strand (2), and pull it back through the loop created at your thumb (3). **(1c)**

step 4 Release the wire from your thumb and tighten the new stitch by separating both strands and pulling them away from the needle with an even tension. **(1d)**

Adding Beads to the LTCO

To add a bead when using this cast-on, keep all beads slipped down the live end so they rest against the spool. Before each cast-on stitch, slip a bead to the needle and hold it with your right thumb while working the next cast-on stitch, which will secure it in place against the needle.

Wire Cast-On (WCO)

Nancie Wiseman, a pioneer in knitting with wire, created a cast-on that uses one wire folded so that a tail is incorporated into the cast-on. I've developed a modified version of this cast-on for the Rose Pin (page 78).

A cousin to the LTCO, the WCO is started in the same way by folding the wire to create a tail.

Preparation

Fold the wire over the needle at the point where the tail begins with both the tail and the live end (attached to the spool) toward you.

Instructions

step 1 Wrap the tail around the live end from the front to the back. **(2a)**

step 2 Wrap the live end around the needle from the back to the front. **(2b)**

Repeat these two steps until the desired number of stitches are cast on. **(2c + 2d)**

Adding Beads to the WCO

To add a bead when using this cast-on, keep all beads slipped down the live end so they rest by the spool until they are needed. Cast on as designated above, but add a third step:

step 3 Slip a bead up to the needle, holding it with your finger until the tail wraps around under the bead, securing it in place against the needle. **(2e)**

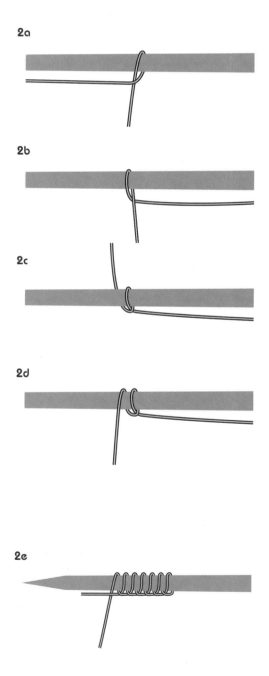

2a

2b

2c

2d

2e

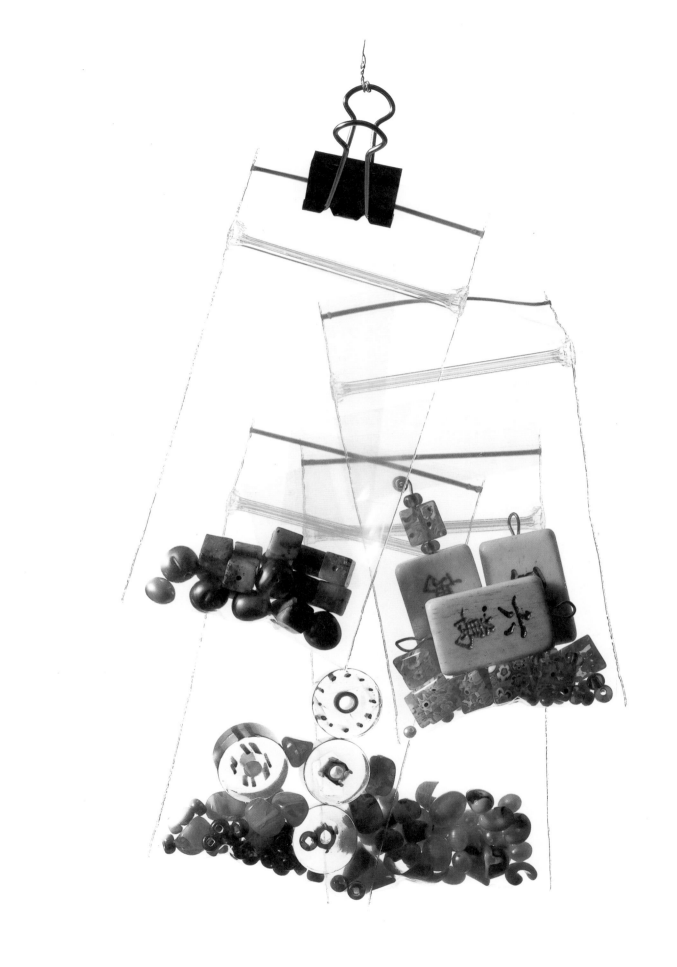

E-Loop or Backward Loop Cast-On

The simple e-loop cast-on is what most knitters learn as their first cast-on; it can also be used in wire knitting. This cast-on provides a very loose edging that may be desirable in certain pieces. The effect, however, can be rather messy and is not appropriate if a more uniform look is desired.

Instructions

step 1 Make a slip knot near the end of the wire. Holding the live end of the wire in your palm with your fingers, stick your thumb out as though you were hitchhiking. **(3a)**

step 2 Wrap the yarn around the thumb in a counterclockwise direction. Slide your needle up the side of your thumb and slip the loop off onto the needle. **(3b + 3c)**

Cable Cast-On

A cable cast-on, or its cousin the knit-on cast-on, are also interesting ways to work your stitches onto the needle. They should be pursued with an alternative fiber before being attempted with wire.

Instructions

step 1 Make a slip knot near the end of the wire. Knit loosely into this knot but do not slip it off the needle.

step 2 Slip the loop just created onto the end of the needle so it rests next to the last stitch.**(4a)**

step 3 Insert the needle between the stitch just created and the next stitch on the needle. Pull a loop through this space as if you were making a knit stitch. **(4b)**

step 4 Repeat the last two steps until the desired number of stitches are on the needle. **(4c)**

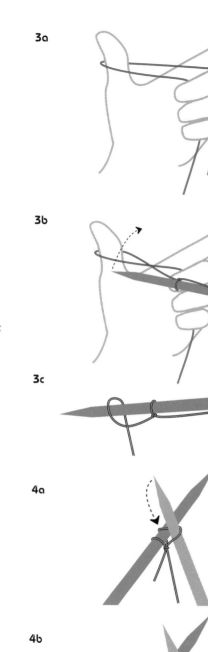

3a

3b

3c

4a

4b

4c

Knit-On Cast-On

Instructions

step 1 Make a slip knot near the end of the wire. Knit loosely into this knot but do not slip it off the needle.

step 2 Slip the loop just created onto the end of the needle so it rests next to the last stitch.

step 3 Knit loosely into the stitch just created; do not slip it off the needle.

Whichever cast-on method you use, it is vital to cast on using a needle at least one size larger, or cast onto two knitting needles at one time, pulling one needle out when the cast-on is complete. Wire has no elasticity, so casting on with the same size needle as you will be using for the piece will lead to very tight tension and may cause breakage.

After casting on, I find it's helpful to wind the extra wire tail around the needle to create a spring that will stay out of the way. This spring can be straightened later for use in finishing your piece. Always leave at least a 5-inch (13cm) tail. That extra wire will come in handy when you're attaching findings!

Making Stitches

Wire will hold its shape, so if a needle falls out it is easy to slip the stitches right back on. However, ripping out is often useless, as the wire becomes so bent and crimped in the process that it is unusable. Drawing the wire through the smoothing pliers can help this, but bear in mind that each time the wire is knit, ripped out, and bent, it weakens substantially.

Dealing with Large Edge Stitches

As with traditional knitting, often the first stitch of a row can grow into a large, unsightly loop. Not every knitter has this problem, but if you do you can simply slip the first stitch of each row to the right-hand needle, not working it, to help

THREE SECRETS OF KNITTING WITH WIRE

1 If you learn nothing else from this book, here is the nut that I hope you take away with you: You will find it easier to master (or mistress) wire knitting if you exaggerate your movements. Wire lacks the elasticity of animal and plant fibers, so it's necessary to make up for this by working larger than you normally would. I tell my students to think of it this way: Imagine that you are teaching someone how to knit. Make your movements broad and exaggerated.

Forcing your hands to move in an overstated manner will initially lead to looser stitches than you might like—don't fret, this is a learning experience! Work as if you were knitting in slow motion and on needles that are several times larger than you have in your hand. Stick with it, work at least 8 rows in this manner, and you'll begin to find a rhythm and tension to create the fabric you desire. Experiment with different knitting needle sizes as you work to determine what feels best in your hands.

2 One of the most useful tips I give my students is to separate their needles from each other after the new stitch is wrapped around the needle. Think of it this way: After you insert your right-hand needle into the next stitch and wrap the wire around the right-hand needle, separate the needles from each other. This will make it easier to pull the new stitch out of the old stitch.

3 This last tip has more to do with setting the tension. I understand that many knitters don't really care if they have a uniform tension when knitting with wire—to be honest, some of the most beautiful pieces I've seen are loose and tight and loose all in the same row.

However, if you would like to achieve a uniform tension in a knit wire piece, here is my best advice: After inserting your right-hand needle into the left-hand stitch, give the wire a gentle tug, thus setting the tension on the last stitch previously worked.

Finish your stitch as you normally would, being careful to pull the needles gently apart as you pull the new stitch through, without worrying about holding the wire tight to the set tension. The tension on the stitch you are currently working will be set when you insert the needle in the next stitch.

This is the rhythm you should strive for: Insert needle, tug to tighten, wrap the wire, separate the needles, pull the stitch out. Make it into a little dance—in, tug, wrap, separate, pull, cha-cha-cha, repeat! You will find that this helps you develop a more regular tension on the wire pieces that demand a little more uniformity. The worst that will happen is you have a little fun.

tighten the edge. Bear in mind that this could tighten your edges more firmly than you'd like, so try experimenting with a wire swatch before working an entire piece using this method!

Beads

Adding a bead to wire knitting is a little different than beading with an animal or plant fiber. Because wire will hold its shape, a bead may move freely along the wire—rather like the wood and wire "roller coaster" toys that enthrall children for hours. A bead will most naturally want to rest on the bar between two purl stitches, and for this reason beads are easier to see in reverse stockinette stitch fabric (the "purl" side of your work).

When you try to force beads to sit within a knit stitch, they have an interesting—and at times infuriating—habit of traveling far away from the intended stitch. For this reason it's generally the best policy to let the bead have its way and seat it in a purl stitch.

Wire knitting is so open that in stockinette stitch fabric it's sometimes hard to tell the knit side from the purl side, so in most cases this point is moot.

To knit a bead into a stitch, work to the point just past where you'd like the bead to rest.

step 1 Insert your needle into the next stitch.
step 2 Slide the bead along the wire to the needle.
step 3 Hold the bead in place with your right index finger.
step 4 Wrap the wire to create the stitch and pull the loop through.

The bead will be resting on the purl bar between the last two stitches worked.

Knitting a bead into a stitch

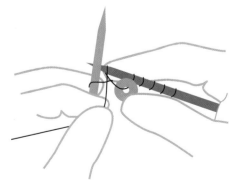

Increasing

When working with wire, due to the nature of knit wire fabric, increases generally won't be very visible. However, when working with finer wire on smaller needles, increases can be prominent.

The easiest way to increase with wire is the lovely **yarn over (yo)**. Simply wrap the wire around the needle before inserting it into the next stitch, then on the following row knit into the leading edge of the yo for an open eyelet, or knit into the trailing edge of the yo for a closed, less visible increase.

Another increase that I like very much—and is a bit more invisible than the yo increase—is what I call the **grandma increase**. Here's my explanation of it—with apologies to all the male knitters out there!

If we think of each row of stitches as a generation, then the row of stitches that currently sits on the needle is the mommy generation. It follows that the row below this row is the grandma generation. The row below the grandma row is the great-grandma generation, all the way down to the original slip knot—Mother Eve.

To work this increase, slip your right-hand needle directly into the center of the stitch immediately below the next stitch on the left-hand needle. Stab the needle straight through; don't try to slip it under, just stick it in. Wrap the wire around the needle and pull a stitch out, then work the stitch above the stitch you've just worked (the next stitch on the needle) and slip off that stitch. This increase can be worked as a knit OR a purl.

This increase will slant to the right, so if you want to match increases (left slanting and right slanting) work half the increases in a right-side row—these will slant to the right; and the other half of the increases in the wrong-side row—these will slant to the left.

Yo increase shown symbolically in a chart as:

M1 increase (grandma increase) shown symbolically in a chart as:

Grandma increase

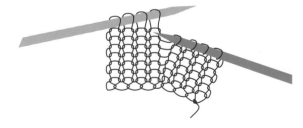

K2tog-R

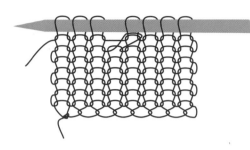

K2tog-R shown symbolically in a chart as:

Creating the k2tog-R

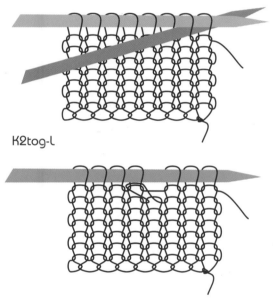

K2tog-L

K2tog-L shown symbolically in a chart as:

Creating the k2tog-L

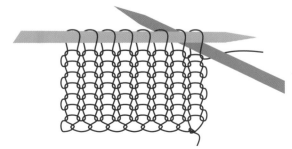

Decreasing

Working stitches together with wire is much the same as in traditional fiber knitting. The main difference is that it is very difficult to see which direction a decrease is slanting, so it's generally not something to lose sleep over. However, we're knitters, and we DO lose sleep over these things.

Knit 2 Together, Left & Right Slanting

I'll be referring to decreases as **k2tog-L** and **k2tog-R** in the course of this book. This is a finer point that may not matter to many knitters, but for those who do care about slanting decreases (or who knit differently than the mainstream) designating decreases as slanting to the left or to the right can make all the difference between creating beautiful lace or lace that looks a little unbalanced.

The traditional Western k2tog will slant to the right, so I call this a k2tog-R.

It's created by inserting the right-hand needle into the front loop of the second stitch on the left-hand needle, then into the front loop of the first stitch from the front, knitwise, and working both together.

The k2tog tbl (or ssk, or skp) will slant to the left, so in this book it will be called k2tog-L.

It's created by inserting the right-hand needle into the back loop of the first stitch on the left-hand needle, then into the back loop of the second stitch through the back loop, knitwise, and working both together. It helps with this decrease to reposition the stitches to be decreased so they are "facing" the point of the left-hand needle if they're not already oriented that way.

Multiple Slanting Decrease

When decreasing three or more stitches in wire, I find it difficult to work my needle into several stitches at a time. Here is a way to make the wire work a bit easier when decreasing multiple stitches.

K3tog-R shown symbolically in a chart as:

Multiple Right-Slanting Decrease

Knit the first stitch, slip it back onto the left-hand needle, then pull the 2nd (and 3rd, 4th, etc.) over the first stitch one by one. Some folks prefer to slip the 2nd, 3rd, and 4th stitch over the first stitch, then knit that first stitch. It's a personal preference.

K3tog-L shown symbolically in a chart as:

Multiple Left-Slanting Decrease

Slip all of the decreasing stitches onto the right-hand needle except for the last stitch, which is knit. One by one pass each of the slipped stitches over the knitted stitch, creating a decrease that slants to the left.

VDD shown symbolically in a chart as:

Vertical Double Decrease (VDD)

A decrease that slants neither to the left nor to the right is called a vertical decrease. The basic three-stitch **VDD** (vertical double decrease) is worked as follows: Slip two stitches off the left-hand needle as if to k2tog-R, knit the next stitch on the left-hand needle, then pass the two slipped stitches over the knit stitch. This will create a beautiful decrease that stands straight.

Blocking on the Needle

After you've worked a few rows, you may be disappointed with the look of your knitted wire. **(5a, page 104)** Like any knit fabric, blocking is required to bring out the beauty of knit wire fabric (yes, fabric!). Blocking is simply any method whereby fabric is cajoled into its final shape. In the case of wire knitting, I find this method works best:

Sliding semiprecious stones and pearls down wire is a peaceful, meditative, almost hypnotic activity. The dyed pears strung in semigraduated sizes shown left will create a pattern in the finished piece like the one in the Blue Velvet Pearl Choker (page 46).

Instructions

step 1 Work at least 3–5 rows, then, grasping the cast-on edge firmly, pull the finished rows as hard as you can away from the needle on which they sit. If your work is long, you may want to thread a separate knitting needle through each stitch in the cast-on row and then pull the two needles apart. **(5b)**

step 2 Grasping the sides of the knit fabric, pull the finished piece widthwise. **(5c)**

Repeat these last two steps several times. You will notice that the stitches begin to even out as they stretch, and your work will take on the appearance of knit fabric.

With some wire you may need to block on the needle every few rows in order to have enough room to work the next row—wire can curl up on itself like any other knit fabric!

Be sure to block your pieces on the needle before binding off. It's good to take advantage of the aluminum needle to provide a firm edge to pull against. Blocking on the needle is only one step, though. You must also block your piece off the needle after binding off.

Binding Off

Binding off isn't as crucial in wire knitting as it is in knitting other fibers. In fact, some very attractive designs use the last row of knit stitches as threading loops for ribbon or heavy elastic cord and don't have a bound-off edge at all!

The traditional Western bind-off (slip a stitch, knit a stitch, pass the slipped stitch over the knit stitch, repeat) can work well with wire, but may not create the most attractive bound-off edge. Here are four alternative bind-offs that reduce total manipulation of the wire.

5a

5b

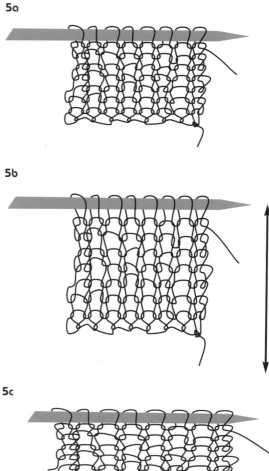

5c

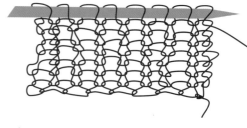

Pulled-Loop Bind-Off

Preparation
Work the last row before the bind-off on a needle at least two sizes larger than previously used. Slip all stitches onto a smaller needle so that the loose end of the wire is near the blunt end of the needle.

Pull the second stitch in from the end through the last stitch on the needle. Slip that stitch back onto the needle so that it becomes the new last stitch and repeat to the end of the row. Pull the wire through the last loop, leaving at least an 8-inch (20cm) tail of wire. This is generally much easier to accomplish with a crochet hook.

Knit 2 Together Bind-Off

Preparation
If they're not already seated this way, turn all stitches so the leading edge is facing toward the point of the needle. They will look as though they want to be knit through their back loop.

K2tog with a left slant, slip the stitch created back onto the left needle, and repeat. Work to the end and pull the wire tail through the last loop.

Knit 2 together bind-off works well in conjunction with the Combination Method of knitting and creates a decorative edge when worked with wire plus a ribbon fiber together.

Twisted Bind-Off

Instructions
Slip the next stitch off the needle, grasp the loop firmly and twist it several times. Be sure to slip the stitches one at a time off the needle to keep the bind-off uniform.

Nancie Wiseman mentions this wonderful bind-off in her book, **Knitting with Wire**. It works beautifully with heavier gauge wire or wire that is being knit very tightly.

Non-Bind-Off Bind-Off

Instructions
Leave the loops on the needle. Slip a ribbon through all the loops. Use the tail of the wire to secure one side of the ribbon to one edge of the work. Use a second piece of wire to secure the other side of the ribbon to the other edge by wrapping the wire around and around the ribbon where it meets the knit piece. (Note: Be sure to do this AFTER you've adjusted the tightness of the ribbon in the piece!)

This is a wonderful bind-off for pieces that require a more delicate finish.

CHAPTER 6

CROCHETING WITH WIRE

I find crocheting with wire more satisfying on many levels than knitting with wire because of the free-form, sculptural nature of crochet. Crochet is well suited to wire because, unlike knitting, binding off is not necessary. Each stitch is bound off as you work it.

This means, though, that wire-crocheted fabric is denser and has more layers than knit fabric of similar dimensions. More wire is required for a wire-crocheted object than for a matching knit one.

As with knitting, the best advice for crocheting with a stiff fiber like wire is to overemphasize your movements, as if you were showing a child how to crochet. In exaggerating the movements, you will give the wire more room in the stitches, thus creating a certain flexibility that is not normally found in wire.

The worst mistake you can make when you start a wire-crocheted project is to work too tightly. Err on the side of working too loosely until you develop a feeling for the slickness of the wire.

Most wire-crocheted pieces start with a simple chain, which you make the same way you work with a plant or animal fiber. It's helpful to use a crochet hook one or two sizes larger than the size specified for the piece when chaining, as it's easy to work a chain a bit too tightly.

Chaining

The first step to most crochet pieces is to create a chain of stitches. To make a chain, just follow these steps:

step 1 Make a slip knot, then insert the crochet hook into the loop of the slip knot. **(6a)**

step 2 Holding both the tail and the live end of the yarn in your left hand, wrap the live end around the hook and pull this loop through the slip knot loop. **(6b)**

step 3 You have just created a chain stitch. **(6c)**

step 4 Repeat steps 1 & 2 to create a chain of stitches. **(6d)**

Single Crochet

After creating a crochet chain, work one more stitch and, skipping this stitch, insert the hook into the second stitch from the hook and follow these instructions:

step 1 Draw a loop of yarn through this stitch. There will now be 2 loops on the hook. **(7a)**

step 2 Wrap the yarn around the hook and draw this loop through both loops already on the hook.

Repeat steps 1 & 2 with each stitch, working back to the original slip knot.

Next row: Turn work, make 1 chain st (ch 1) and repeat steps 1 & 2 across the work, inserting the hook into both loops of each stitch from the previous row.

Making a chain

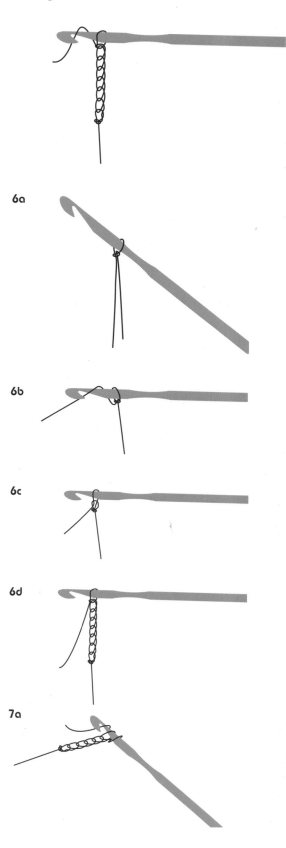

6a

6b

6c

6d

7a

Single, Double & Treble Crochet

Single crochets are relatively easy to work in wire, but double and treble crochets require so much manipulation that it can lead to breakage. These stitches are best left to animal and plant fibers, or worked with very thin wire stranded with a crochet thread.

Chaining & Beads

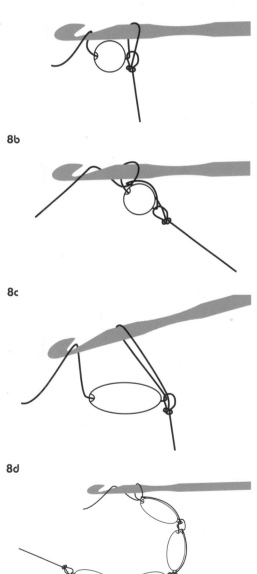

8a

8b

8c

8d

Amazing pieces can be made by chaining alone, or by marrying a crocheted chain with beads (see Three-Strand Very Simple Crocheted Necklace on page 18, Chain Flower Pin on page 74, and Chain Shell Necklace page 16). The way you slip the bead onto the hook and hold it will determine where the bead sits on the finished piece. Slipping a bead onto the hook before each chain will nest that bead into the center of the chain stitch. **(8a)** When worked with a very large crochet hook, the beads retain their mobility, slipping back and forth across the loops and giving the piece a lovely, fluid effect.

Slip a bead onto the hook and yarn over. **(8b)** Then draw the yarn over through the loop to secure the bead in place. **(8c)**

When working with very long beads, be sure to draw the loop so that it is as long as the bead, as shown here and in the Chain Shell Necklace (page 52). Otherwise, the bead will not lay flat against the chain, which can be a problem if you're creating a necklace. **(8d)**

CHAPTER 7

FINISHING WIRE PIECES

Finishing is the process whereby your raw piece becomes jewelry. In many ways this is most important step, the point when you take care of loose wire ends and attach findings to make your piece wearable.

When creating your jewelry, make sure to leave at least a 5-inch (13cm) tail after binding off. This will be useful later in attaching findings or finishing the piece.

Even though you're working with wire, you still need to block. You'll have to pull harder than you might first imagine, first widthwise, then lengthwise, while the piece is still on the needle. With each pull and tug, you'll see your work evening out, the stitches becoming more uniform, and the whole piece becoming more visually appealing.

Blocking Off the Needle

Once your piece is bound-off, it may not have the shape that you desire. Wire is nothing if not malleable, so it's relatively easy to form your masterpiece into the shape you desire. Take the time to pull the cast-on and bound-off edges away from each other, then pull the sides apart. Repeat this several times, as when the piece was on the needle, but now if the piece wants to curve into a three-dimensional shape, it will be easier to accommodate it.

Findings

Findings are the small bits used in jewelry making that help finish the piece in a useful way. A finding can be an earring hook, a clasp, a closure, or a metal spacer that rests between beads (see page 89 for examples). Beautiful findings can finish a piece, but rough, unbalanced, or poorly made findings can make even the nicest wire knitting look shoddy.

You can discover many beautiful findings at craft or bead stores. All the findings used in the jewelry featured in this book were purchased from national chain stores. However, if you'd like to try making your own findings, you'll find that with a little practice and the right tools you can create a perfect accent for your jewelry piece.

For an excellent reference on creating your own findings, see **Findings & Finishings** by Sharon Bateman (Interweave Press, 2003).

BASIC FINISHING TERMS

There are several basic wire finishing terms that are used in this book to explain specific techniques.

Twisting

Twisting is the process whereby two or more strands of wire are twisted together, forming a tight double (or triple) strand. You can twist wires with your hands, but pliers make a much more even twisted cord. Three wires will twist more evenly than two wires, and will give the piece a nicer finish.

Spiraling

Spiraled wire makes a lovely decorative end for an eye pin and is useful in wire finishing. Turn a single wire or a group of twisted wires in concentric circles to form a flat piece. Bend the end of the wire, then use the flat edge of a pair of pliers to rotate the bend to create a spiral.

Coiling

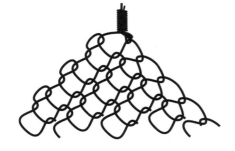

Coiled wire is useful for making springs and jump rings, and in finishing. When finishing a piece, coiling is a good alternative to spiraling if the wire is very thin.

Wrap the wire around a knitting needle or the end of a pair of round-nose pliers until the desired length is reached.

Wrapping

Wrapping can be decorative or purely utilitarian. It can be used to connect several pieces of wire together, or to simply add a nice touch to an edge. Try wrapping wire around a necklace ribbon at the point where the wire and ribbon meet as a decorative way to finish a piece.

Wrapping can be used, in conjunction with twisting and spiraling, to secure findings (hook and eyes) to the ends of a necklace or bracelet.

Moving Wires into Position

When starting the finishing process, it helps if you're able to weave the wires so that both the bind-off and cast-on ends of the wire are positioned in an inconspicuous place. For instance, when making a cuff bracelet, I like to weave my wires to the center of the wrong side of the cuff. When making a necklace, I like to weave each wire end up to the point where the wire meets the attaching ribbon, or near a closure. Each piece will be different, and it's important to use your discretion in finding appropriate places to hide the finished wire ends.

Finishing Loose Wires

This may seem daunting, but if you approach it step by step, it simplifies the process:

step 1 Pull the loose wire end(s) through the piece, creating a loop and a tail (resembling the number six). **(8a + 8b)**

step 2 Using pliers, twist the loop and the single tail together, creating a 3-strand twist that is at least ⅝ inch (1.6cm) long. Use your wire cutters to shorten the piece to ½ inch (1.3cm). **(8c)**

step 3 Coil this twisted strand and crimp it (press it very tightly) against the inside of the piece. As you press the spiral in the pliers, be careful not to inadvertently squeeze any beads, which can break.

TIP: After coiling the twisted loose ends of wire and crimping in place, it's sometimes helpful to add a dot of clear nail polish to the crimped area to prevent skin irritation from a loose wire end.

8a

8b

8c

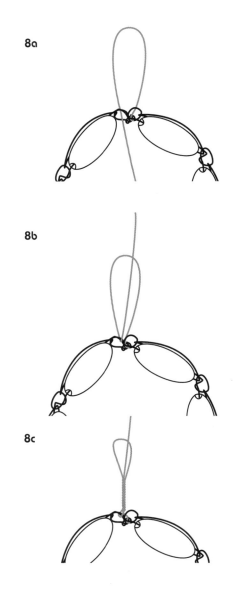

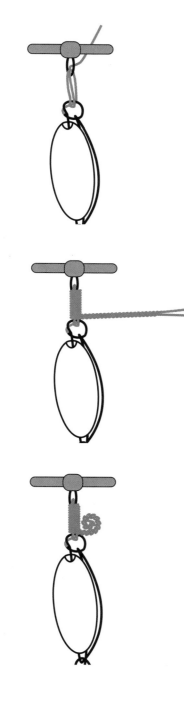

9a

9b

9c

Attaching Findings

Findings must be attached so that the join is not only beautiful, but strong.

step 1 Pull the attaching wires through the end of the piece and then through the loop of the finding.

step 2 Insert a knitting needle between the wires. Pass the end of one wire through the edge of the piece, then back through the loop of the finding, around the knitting needle, several times, creating a ring of wires. Remove the knitting needle from the ring, leaving a space between the finding and the edge of the piece. **(9a)**

Pull the ring taut to increase the space between the finding and the edge of the piece. Lay the shorter wire along the stretched ring.

step 3 Wrap the longer wire around the group of wires, moving toward the edge of the piece. **(9b)**

step 4 At the edge of the piece, twist the two wires together, then coil the twisted wire. **(9c)**

step 5 Lay the coil against the wrapped wire and crimp it tightly together. Add a drop of clear nail polish if there are rough edges.

CHAPTER 9 RESOURCES

You can never have too many resources—especially the name of a good wire supplier or a clear explanation for a tricky stitch. Although all efforts were made to create a complete resource section, there may be changes in some of this information or new suppliers popping up in the next few years. My best advice is to perform regular internet searches to find new sources for wire, tools, and wire-working books and techniques.

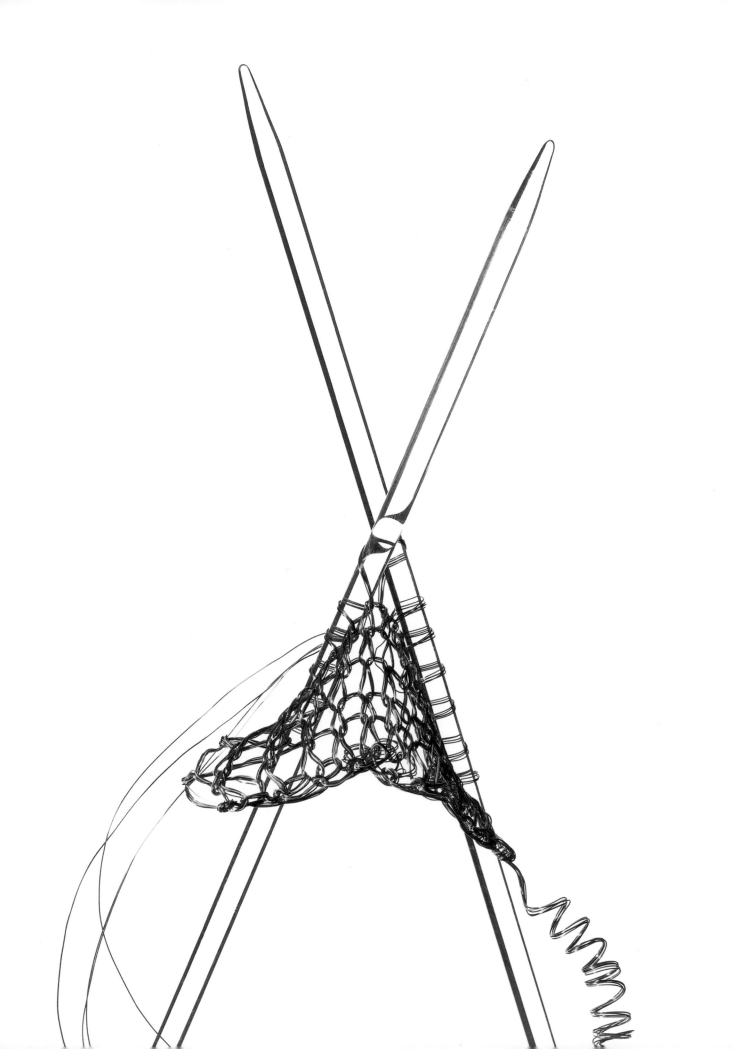

GLOSSARY OF STITCHES

bc—bead crochet
Insert hook in stitch, push bead up the thread as close to work as possible, yarn over, draw loop through, yarn over, draw loop through the two loops on hook.

BO—bind off

ch—chain

dangle tiles
Use the flat edge of a pair of pliers to coil the end of a 3½" piece of 22 gauge red wire, press the coil tightly to harden it. Slip 1 red bead, 1 square bead, 1 red bead, and 1 tile onto the wire. Wrap the top of the wire over a knitting needle and insert the end back into the tile, pushing it as far as it will go. Twist the top loop several times to tighten.

dc—double crochet
Yarn over hook, insert hook in the next stitch to be worked, yarn over hook, draw through stitch, yarn over hook, draw through first 2 loops on hook, yarn over hook, draw through remaining 2 loops on hook.

double loop tiles
Create loops on either end of 7 tiles by folding a 2½" piece of 22 gauge red wire onto itself so the ends meet in the middle. Insert this folded piece through the tile and use a knitting needle to open the ends. Holding both ends of the wire, twist several times to lock together the wire inside the tile.

hdc—half double crochet
Yarn over hook. Insert hook in the next stitch to be worked. Yarn over hook. Pull yarn through stitch. Yarn over hook. Pull yarn through all 3 loops on hook (one half double crochet made).

k2tog BO preparation
If they're not already seated this way, turn all stitches so the leading edge is facing toward the point of the needle. They will look as if they want to be knit through their back loop. K2tog with a left slant (k2tog-L), slip the stitch created back onto the left needle, and repeat. Work to the end and pull the wire tail through the last loop.

k2tog-L—knit 2 together with a left slant (AKA ssk, k2tog-tbl, and skp)
Knit 2 stitches together so they slant to the left when viewed from right side of work

k2tog-R—knit 2 together with a right slant (AKA k2tog)
Knit 2 stitches together so they slant to the right when viewed from right side of work.

k3tog—knit 3 together (multiple slanting decrease)
Knit 3 stitches together, pulling 1 loop from all three stitches. This decrease can slant either to the left or to the right depending on whether you insert your needle into the 1st, then 2nd, then 3rd stitch on the needle (left slant) or into the 3rd, then 2nd, then 1st stitch on the needle (right slant).

knit bead
Slide bead to needle and hold in place with right thumb or index finger, work 1 knit stitch. Bead will rest on section of wire that runs between two knit stitches and will be most visible from the reverse stockinette stitch side of piece.

non-bind-off bind off
Leave the loops on the needle. Slip a ribbon through all of the loops. Use the tail of the wire to secure one side of the ribbon to one edge of the work, use a

second piece of wire to secure the other side of the ribbon to the other edge by wrapping the wire around and around the ribbon where it meets the knit piece. (Note: Be sure to do this AFTER you've adjusted the tightness of the ribbon in the piece.)

pulled-loop bind-off preparation

Work the last row before the bind-off on a needle at least 2 sizes larger than previously used. Slip all stitches onto a smaller needle so that the loose end of the wire is near the blunt end of the needle. Pull the second stitch in from the end through the last stitch on the needle. Slip that stitch back on the needle so that it becomes the new last stitch and repeat to the end of the row. Pull the wire through the last loop, leaving at least an 8" tail of wire. This is generally much easier to accomplish with a crochet hook.

sc—single crochet

Insert hook in stitch. Yarn over hook. Pull yarn through stitch. Yarn over hook. Pull yarn through 2 loops on hook (one single crochet made).

sc2tog—single crochet 2 together

Insert hook into next stitch, yarn over, draw loop through (2 loops on hook) then insert hook into next stitch, yarn over, draw loop through (3 loops on hook), yarn over, draw loop through all stitches on hook.

sl st—slip stitch

Slip crochet hook into stitch, yarn over, draw loop through stitch and through loop on hook.

slipped BO

Slip all stitches to small needle so the stitch with the yarn attached is the last stitch on needle. Using either a knitting needle or crochet hook, slip 2nd stitch on needle through 1st stitch on needle. Slip next stitch

on needle through loop just created. Continue in this fashion until all stitches are bound off, pulling fiber through last stitch.

square dangle

Use the flat edge of a pair of pliers to coil the end of a 3½" piece of 22 gauge copper wire, press the coil tightly to harden it. Slip 1 silver-lined gold bead, 1 square bead, 2 silver lined gold beads onto the wire. Coil the top of the wire to create a hanging loop. Crimp flat to harden loop.

VDD—vertical double decrease

Slip 2 stitches as if to work k2tog, knit 1, pass slipped stitches over (decrease 2 stitches).

W&T—wrap & turn

Slip next stitch to right-hand needle, wrap yarn around stitch, and return to left-hand needle. Turn work and begin working back in the opposite direction from the previous row.

yo—yarn over

Wrap yarn around hook or needle.

YYK—yarn over, yarn over, knit

Slip right-hand needle into stitch as if to knit, wrap yarn twice around right-hand needle. Next row: Only work 1st loop in this stitch, allowing yarn over to drop, which creates an extra-long stitch.

SUPPLIERS

All of the projects in this book call for materials and notions that are widely distributed at yarn, beading, and craft stores near you. The list below will help you find any jewelry-making supplies, beads, yarns, or needles and hooks you may need to complete the projects. You can go to the company's website to locate the store nearest you. If the resource is only online, that is indicated too.

Craft Stores & Jewelry Supply

Allcraft Jewelry Supply
212-297-7077
www.allcraftonline.com
(online retailer)

Jewelry Supply.com
866-380-7464
www.jewelrysupply.com
(online retailer)

Jo-Ann Fabric & Crafts
818-739-4120
www.joann.com
(store locator available)

Michaels Craft Stores
800-642-4235
www.michaels.com
(store locator available)

Rag Shop
973-423-1303
www.ragshop.com
(store locator available)

Treasure Island
800-648-0109
www.treasureislandstores.com
(store locator available)

Wire

All the projects in this book call for Artistic Wire, but you can purchase other brands at the sources listed at left.

Artistic Wire
630-530-7567
www.artisticwire.com
(store locator available)

Beads & Findings

Most of the projects in this book call for one or several specific brands of beads. Listed below is information on where to buy specific brands, along with a few of my other favorite retailers.

Ambrosia Arts
360-385-1625
www.ambrosiaarts2.com
(online retailer)

Ancient Moon Beads
617-926-1887
www.ancientmoonbeads.com
(order online or visit their
Watertown, MA, location)

The Bead Hut
864-226-BEAD
www.thebeadhut.com
(order online or visit their
Anderson, SC, location)

Blue Moon Beads
800-377-6715
www.bluemoonbeads.com
(products are widely distributed, or call
them directly for a distributor near you)

J & M Gems
201-585-5398
www.orientbeads.com
(online retailer)

Just Bead It
973-403-7675
www.justbeadit.net
(order online or shop at NJ locations)

Multi Creations NJ, Inc.
www.multicreationsnj.com
(online retailer)

Tender Buttons
212-758-7004
(locations in New York and Chicago)

Veni Vidi Beadi
640-459-9490
www.venividibeadi.com
(online retailer)

Yarn & Ribbons
Artyarns
914-428-0333
www.artyarns.com
(retailer locator available)

Crystal Palace Yarns
510-237-9988 | 510-237-9809
www.crystalpalaceyarns.com
(products are widely distributed)

Habu Textiles
212-239-3546
www.habutextiles.com
(products are widely distributed)

Halcyon Yarn
800-341-0282
www.halcyonyarn.com
(order online or visit them in Bath, ME)

Himalaya Yarn
802-862-6985
www.himalayayarn.com
(retailer locator available)

Mokuba Ribbon
212-869-8900
www.mokubany.com
(products are widely distributed—try
www.florilegium.com for a good online retailer)

Steinlauf & Stoller, Inc
212-869-0321
www.steinlaufandstoller.com
(call or e-mail to place an order)

Knitting Needles & Crochet Hooks
Boye Aluminum
Needles & Hooks
www.wrights.com
(retailer locator available)

Namaste Glass Needles
818-363-9853
www.namasteneedles.com
(retailer locator available)

Susan Bates Aluminum
Needles & Hooks
www.coatsandclark.com
(retailer locator available)

FOR FURTHER READING

If you wish to learn more about jewelry making or knitting with wire, here are some suggestions for further reading.

Confessions of a Knitting Heretic
Annie Modesitt
South Orange, NJ: ModeKnit Press, 2004

Creative Knitting: A New Art Form
Mary Walker Phillips
New York: Van Nostrand Reinhold, 1980

Crochet with Wire
Nancie Wiseman
Loveland, CO: Interweave Press, 2005

The Encyclopedia of Jewelry-Making
Techniques: A Comprehensive Visual Guide
to Traditional and Contemporary Techniques
Jinks McGrath
Philadelphia: Running Press, 1995

Findings and Finishing: A Beadwork
How-To Book
Sharon Bateman
Loveland, CO: Interweave Press, 2003

Knitting for Anarchists
Anna Zilboorg
Petaluma, CA: Unicorn Books & Crafts, 2002

Knitting in the Old Way: Designs and
Techniques from Ethnic Sweaters
Priscilla A. Gibson-Roberts
White River Junction, VT: Nomad Press, 2004

Knitting with Wire
Nancie Wiseman
Loveland, CO: Interweave Press, 2003

The Potter Needlework Library: Beading
Diana Vernon
New York: Potter Craft, 2006

Silver Wire Jewelry:
Projects to Coil, Braid & Knit
Irene From Peterson
Asheville, NC: Lark Books, 2005

Simply Pearls: Designs for Creating
Perfect Pearl Jewelry
Nancy Alden
New York: Potter Craft, 2006

Textile Techniques in Metal
Arline M. Fisch
Asheville, NC: Lark Books, 2001

Woven Wire Jewelry: Contemporary
Designs and Creative Techniques
Christine Ritchey & Linda L. Chandler
Loveland, CO: Interweave Press, 2004

INDEX